Getting Started in a
Pharmacy
Residency

Notice

Getting Started in a
Pharmacy Residency

Monica L. Miller, PharmD, MSc

Clinical Assistant Professor of Pharmacy Practice
College of Pharmacy
Purdue University
West Lafayette, Indiana

Adjunct Assistant Professor
School of Medicine
Indiana University
Indianapolis, Indiana

American Pharmacists Association®
Improving medication use. Advancing patient care.

APhA

Washington, D.C.

Managing and Content Editor: Vicki Meade, Meade Communications
Acquiring Editor: Sandra Cannon
Assistant Copy Editor: Paula Novash
Proofreaders: Betty Bruner and Mary De Angelo
Indexer: Jennifer Burton, Columbia Indexing Group
Cover Designer: Scott Neitzke, APhA Creative Services
Layout and Graphics: Michele A. Danoff, Graphics by Design

© 2013 by the American Pharmacists Association
APhA was founded in 1852 as the American Pharmaceutical Association.

Published by the American Pharmacists Association
2215 Constitution Avenue, NW
Washington, DC 20037-2985
www.pharmacist.com   www.pharmacylibrary.com

To comment on this book via email, send your message to the publisher at
aphabooks@aphanet.org

Library of Congress Cataloging-in-Publication Data

Getting started in a pharmacy residency / [edited by] Monica L. Miller.
       p. ; cm.
   Includes bibliographical references and index.
   ISBN 978-1-58212-155-0
   I. Miller, Monica L. (Monica Lee), 1980- II. American Pharmacists Association.
   [DNLM: 1. Education, Pharmacy, Graduate. 2. Internship, Nonmedical. 3.
Interviews as Topic—methods. 4. Vocational Guidance.   QV 20]

   615.1023—dc23
                              2013001887

How to Order This Book

Online: www.pharmacist.com/shop
By phone: 800-878-0729 (from the United States and Canada)
VISA®, MasterCard®, and American Express® cards accepted

Dedication

To my family: Wayne, Jeanne, and Sheila Miller, and Aaron Marney. Thank you all for the unwavering support over the years.

Contents

Preface

The impetus for this book came from both the APhA publication committee and me. Collectively, we wanted to develop a book that could be used by student pharmacists to help them successfully navigate the entire process of obtaining a pharmacy residency.

When I was going through the residency selection and application process, I remember the stress of not knowing what was expected. Thankfully, I had many mentors and upperclassmen friends who helped educate me. As a faculty member and mentor myself, I work to provide the same insight for students as they go through the process. What I realized when I started working on this book was that students received primarily anecdotal—and very subjective—information. I wanted to apply rigor to the process of writing the book, so I interviewed and surveyed many residency directors and students to discover what obtaining a pharmacy residency is like today. This information is woven into the fabric of each chapter. Coauthors helped me with some of the chapters to ensure that I included well-researched material.

The book is set up to walk you through key steps, including how to connect with program representatives, the application process, the Match, and what to do before you start your residency. It provides helpful sidebars, lists, and reminders you can use in each phase of the process.

It's an informal book; that is, rather than being a dry reference book, it has a conversational tone. You can read it from beginning to end or dip in wherever topics interest you the most. I included quotes and stories from pharmacists who have recently been through the residency process so you can get a feel for their many different experiences—and hear, in their voices, tips to smooth your way. To learn more about the people quoted in the book, see the Contributors section that follows the Preface.

I was motivated to write this book because I wanted to help students have a thorough resource to guide them through the residency or industry fellowship application process. Many websites provide good information, but I hope this book compiles the most salient information in one accessible place.

I wish you all the best on your residency journey, and I hope this book is a helpful companion along the way. Feel free to get in touch and tell me which sections were helpful, what we left out that you wish had been included, and what you learned on your own residency search.

Monica L. Miller
mille355@purdue.edu
February 2013

Contributors

Chapter Coauthors

Mina Alsaraf, PharmD, graduated from Purdue University College of Pharmacy in 2010 and went on to a two-year pharmaceutical industry fellowship in health policy and advocacy with Bristol-Myers Squibb and Rutgers University before becoming a clinical pharmacist with a focus on pharmacoeconomics at Blue Cross Blue Shield of Michigan.

Joseph A. Barone, PharmD, FCCP, is acting dean and professor II for the Ernest Mario School of Pharmacy in Piscataway, New Jersey. After graduating from St. John's University College of Pharmacy in Jamaica, New York, he completed an advanced pharmacy residency in emergency medicine with the Department of Pharmacy Practice at the University of Illinois Medical Center in Chicago. He founded the Rutgers Pharmaceutical Industry Fellowship Program.

Deanna Kania, PharmD, BCPS, is clinical associate professor of pharmacy practice, Purdue University College of Pharmacy, and adjunct assistant professor, School of Health and Rehabilitation Sciences, Indiana University.

Molly A. Mason, PharmD, BCPS, is a clinical pharmacy specialist in emergency medicine at Indiana University Health Methodist Hospital in Indianapolis.

Myra Wooley, PharmD, is a clinical research fellow at Cubist Pharmaceuticals, Inc., in conjunction with the Massachusetts College of Pharmacy and Health Sciences Postdoctoral Fellowship Program.

Interviewees Quoted

Joy Barclay, PharmD, is executive director of HIV Strategy, Global Commercialization, Bristol-Myers Squibb, in Princeton, New Jersey. She received her BS in pharmacy from the Medical University of South Carolina, her PharmD from the Medical College of Virginia, and her executive master's in business administration from Columbia University. She completed a pharmaceutical industry fellowship in internal medicine at the Medical University of South Carolina.

Ed Battjes, PharmD, is a pharmacist at St. Joseph Regional Medical Center in Mishawaka, Indiana. He graduated from Purdue University in 2010 and completed a diabetes-focused, community-based ambulatory care residency in 2011 associated with Purdue University and Mathes Pharmacy.

Amanda Bishop, PharmD, will finish a PGY2 residency in 2013 focused on health administration at Virginia Mason in Seattle, Washington. She graduated from Purdue University in 2011 and completed a PGY1 residency in managed care in 2012 at Providence Health & Services in Portland, Oregon.

Ashley Crumby, PharmD, is clinical assistant professor of pharmacy practice at the College of Pharmacy, Purdue University. She also provides clinical pharmacy services at the Riley Hospital for Children in Indianapolis and the Ryan White Center for Pediatric Infectious Disease at the Indiana University Health Pediatric HIV Clinic. She graduated from the University of Mississippi in 2009 and completed a PGY1 pediatric pharmacy practice residency at Arkansas Children's Hospital in Little Rock in 2010, followed by a PGY2 residency in pediatric infectious diseases at the same institution, which she completed in 2011.

Patty Elsner, PharmD, is an adjunct faculty member in the Department of Pharmacy Practice at the Purdue University College of Pharmacy. She received her PharmD from Purdue in 2001. She is a pharmacy manager in West Lafayette, Indiana, and serves as university advocate for professional development and residency program director for Walgreens.

Caity Frail, PharmD, is a community practice research fellow with the Purdue University College of Pharmacy and is pursuing an MS in pharmacy practice, with a concentration in medication safety. She graduated from the West Virginia University School of Pharmacy in 2009 and in 2010 completed an executive residency in association management at the National Community Pharmacists Association in Alexandria, Virginia.

Isabel Hagedorn, PharmD, earned her degree from Purdue University College of Pharmacy in 2009 and then completed a PGY1 residency at St. Joseph Regional Medical Center in South Bend, Indiana, after which she finished an ambulatory care/public health PGY2 residency at Butler University in Indianapolis. Following residency training in 2011, she pursued a global health fellowship with Purdue University based in Eldoret, Kenya, East Africa.

John Hertig, PharmD, MS, medication safety project manager with the Purdue University College of Pharmacy Center for Medication Safety Advancement, received a BS in pharmaceutical sciences and PharmD from Purdue University in 2008. He completed a combined PGY1/PGY2 Master's in Health-System Pharmacy Administration Residency at The Ohio State University Medical Center in Columbus in 2010, which included an MS in Health-System Pharmacy Administration.

Jennifer Huntington, PharmD, is senior clinical research scientist at Cubist Pharmaceuticals, Inc., in Lexington, Massachusetts. She graduated from the University of Connecticut in 2007 and completed a pharmaceutical industry fellowship at Cubist Pharmaceuticals in 2009.

Ashley Johns, PharmD, is an investigational drug services pharmacist at City of Hope hospital in Duarte, California. She graduated from Western University of Health Sciences in 2005, after which she completed her PGY1 residency with the University of California, Irvine. She went on to complete a PGY2/MS with the University of Texas at Austin and The University of Texas Health Science Center in San Antonio in oncology pharmacy.

Carolyn Jung, PharmD, is an assistant professor of pharmacy practice at Butler University and a clinical pharmacy specialist in internal medicine at Wishard Health Services in Indianapolis. She graduated from Purdue University in 2009 and completed a PGY1 residency at Wishard Health Services in 2010, followed by a PGY2 residency in pharmacotherapy at Community Health Network/Butler University.

Korby Lathrop, PharmD, graduated from the University of Wisconsin – Madison School of Pharmacy in 2011 and then completed a two-year combined pharmacy administration residency and master's in health-system pharmacy degree with the University of Wisconsin Hospital and Clinics.

Tiffany Marsh, PharmD, is regional medical liaison at Sanofi, Inc., with a territory of New York. She graduated from Florida Agricultural and Mechanical University in 2006 and completed a pharmaceutical industry fellowship in Medical Strategy at Bristol-Myers Squibb and Rutgers University in 2007.

Eve McMichael, PharmD, is a clinical pharmacist on the transplant team at IU Health – University Hospital in Indiana, where she focuses on patients who need or have received liver or intestine transplants. She graduated from Butler University in 2005 and was a retail pharmacist at Walgreens before joining University Hospital in Indianapolis as a staff pharmacist, where she continued working while completing a nontraditional PGY1 Pharmacy Practice Residency at IU Health 2010. In 2011 she was the first nontraditional resident to also complete a PGY2 specialty residency, which focused on critical care and trauma, with half her time spent at IU Health – Methodist Hospital and half at Wishard Health Services.

Joshua Raub, PharmD, is a clinical pharmacy specialist in internal medicine at Detroit Receiving Hospital of the Detroit Medical Center, and is also adjunct professor of pharmacy practice at Wayne State University's Eugene Applebaum College of Pharmacy and Health Sciences. He graduated from Wayne State University in 2009 and completed a PGY1 pharmacy practice residency in 2010 at The Johns Hopkins Hospital in Baltimore, Maryland.

Edward P. Sheridan, PharmD, is the pharmacy residency program founder/director and family medicine residency program faculty at St. Joseph Regional Medical Center in Mishawaka, Indiana, where he has practiced ambulatory care medicine since 1996. He earned his bachelor of science in pharmacy and PharmD from Butler University in Indianapolis.

Amanda Slinde, PharmD, graduated from the University of Minnesota College of Pharmacy in 2008 and completed her PGY1 residency at Children's Hospitals and Clinics of Minnesota, where she then worked for 3 years as a pediatric clinical pharmacist. In 2012 she joined the clinical staff in the neonatal and pediatric intensive care units of IU Health Methodist Hospital in Indianapolis.

Colleen Teevan, PharmD, finished a PGY2 residency in critical care at Midwestern University/Northwest Community Hospital in Chicago in 2012 and is now the emergency department clinical pharmacist at The Hospital of Central Connecticut. She graduated from the University of Connecticut in 2010 and completed a PGY1 residency at St. Joseph Regional Medical Center in Mishawaka, Indiana.

Sonia Vainrub, PharmD, will finish a PGY2 residency in internal medicine at The University of Arizona Medical Center in 2013. She graduated from the University of Minnesota in 2011 and completed a PGY1 residency at University of Wisconsin Hospital and Clinics in 2012.

Megan Zolman, PharmD, completed a drug information specialty residency with GlaxoSmithKline and Duke University Hospital in Durham, North Carolina, in 2012. She graduated from Purdue University in 2008 and worked as a staff pharmacist and pharmacy manager at Kroger Pharmacy in Columbus, Ohio, and Durham, North Carolina, before beginning her residency.

Acknowledgments

I would not have been able to write this book without the help of many people. Some contributed directly and are named in the "contributors" section, but many others helped indirectly by telling me a story, giving me an idea, or letting me bounce ideas off them. Others served as my cheering section as I embarked on the adventure of writing this book.

Thank you to my husband, Aaron. You are a constant source of support and love. I appreciate how you know the right thing to say when my spirits get a little low—words that make me laugh and help me get back to work. Thank you for not minding when I worked late into the evening or during weekends. I am so fortunate to have you as my partner.

Thank you to my family (Wayne, Jeanne, and Sheila). You are always there on the other end of the phone to share my joys and sorrows. As I worked on this book, memories came back to me of your support throughout pharmacy school, my residency search, my residency program, and my career. I'm so blessed to have such an amazing support system.

Thank you to my students. You were a constant inspiration as I was writing this book. Each day, as I researched and compiled various sections, I thought of you and the challenges you face in the residency search/selection process. I hope to use what you've taught me to help students in the future.

Thank you to my colleagues and friends. I appreciate your patience with me and your willingness to answer my odd questions, let me pick your brains, and tell me about your residency search processes. Your input inspired my decisions about what to include in this book.

Thank you to everyone who contributed quotes. You entrusted me with your stories and thoughts without really knowing how I would use this information. I'm sorry that I did not have room to use every quote, and I'm grateful for your efforts.

Last of all, thank you to Jan Metzler. You have been a huge support to me throughout my time at Purdue. You are always finding ways to help me, and this book is no exception. You don't bat an eye if I ask you to create a list of residency directors or contact people for head shots and bios. I really appreciate your time and hard work.

Chapter 1

Deciding on Postgraduate Training

By Deanna Kania and Monica L. Miller

Why should you pursue postgraduate training? A key reason is to gain a competitive advantage in the job market by building specialized skills and deepening your experience. Options include completing a pharmacy residency, earning an advanced degree, such as a master's or PhD, or doing a fellowship in an academic health center, the pharmaceutical industry, or other setting where you can pursue in-depth research. Today, residency programs are a popular choice for postgraduate training in pharmacy, with close to 20% of recent graduates enrolling in Postgraduate year 1 (PGY1) residencies.

In the past 20 years, the number of pharmacy residency programs has multiplied tenfold, to more than 1400. Although this number includes both PGY1 and Postgraduate year 2 (PGY2) programs, the majority of programs— roughly 900—are PGY1. New programs are springing up because of demand by employers looking for residency-trained pharmacists, and also because of pharmacy's expanding role in direct patient care services. Many experts believe that eventually all pharmacists who provide direct patient care will be required to complete a residency before entering practice.

The profession of pharmacy continues to grow, reinvent itself, and become more competitive every year. To set myself apart from other pharmacists and job candidates, a residency was the perfect place to start. Additionally, the training that is received throughout the residency year is unmatched. The ability to be exposed to such a variety of practice settings and specialty areas is unique to the experience and cannot be gained in the regular job setting. For me, my residency was the first step toward obtaining career goals.

—Amanda Bishop

Residency training gives you extensive, hands-on experience in working with patients. Sidebar 1-1 provides a detailed summary of important benefits of completing a residency. A few general reasons residencies are worthwhile include the following:

- Building a network of professional contacts and colleagues in your field, which will be an important source of information, support, and career advice for years to come.

- Figuring out what type of practice suits you the best.

- Getting a broader view of the pharmacy profession, learning to work comfortably with other members of the health team, and developing leadership skills.

My Residency Choice

When I (Monica) decided to complete a residency, my reasons were simple: I wanted to gain expertise in caring for patients, learn how to conduct pharmacy practice-based research, and develop my teaching skills. My career goal was to become a clinical faculty member with a college or school of pharmacy.

After searching and interviewing at various programs, I selected a two-year pharmacotherapy residency that met my main objectives—giving me clinical experience and the opportunity to conduct research over a period longer than a year. The program also allowed me to earn a master's of science in pharmacy. I completed the program, offered through The University of Texas Health Science Center in San Antonio and the University of Texas at Austin, in 2008.

I wanted to pursue a career in pharmacy outside the norm of community and hospital staff positions. I was unsure whether I wanted to do clinical work or shift directions entirely to do more administrative/ public health type work. I felt that pursuing a residency would help me gain experience to decide if this career path was right for me and help broaden the options for what my next move would be.

—Isabel Hagedorn

Among the many things my residency program taught me was that I could handle a heavier workload—and more stress—than I thought, which ultimately boosted my confidence for pursuing a clinical faculty member position. It prepared me for the real world by giving me independence

Sidebar 1-1. Benefits of Completing a Residency

Completing a residency program offers many benefits, some of which can be quantified, such as knowledge gained and skills developed. Others are more intangible, such as the relationships you form and the opportunities that become available to you. Below is a list of key benefits.

Improved clinical skills, confidence, and critical thinking. You gain more experience in direct patient care, project development, management, and other activities where you can apply knowledge you learned in the pharmacy curriculum and expand your problem-solving skills.

Competitive advantage in the job market. Many pharmacy positions today, especially those associated with direct patient care, require some level of residency training. Both the American College of Clinical Pharmacy (ACCP) and the American Society of Health-System Pharmacists (ASHP) House of Delegates have indicated that by the year 2020, completing an ASHP-accredited residency should be required of all new college of pharmacy graduates who will be providing direct patient care.[1,2] In some fields a residency is already a prerequisite for a job, and this trend will continue as the job market becomes more competitive. Additionally, as the practice of pharmacy keeps shifting further from a product-oriented profession to one focused on patient care, pharmacy graduates will need to obtain the knowledge, clinical experience, and problem solving, communication, leadership, and interpersonal skills needed to optimize outcomes and excel in managing patients.

More effective teaching. Every day, pharmacists are teachers to patients, caregivers, other health care professionals, students, and colleagues. Residency programs often offer many teaching opportunities, which allow you to become comfortable in teaching roles and adapt to different learners. You may precept student pharmacists completing rotations during pharmacy school, teach didactic lectures, provide continuing education or staff development programs, conduct nursing or physician in-service training, or lead community service activities, such as brown bag lunches or health fairs. You may also have the opportunity to take part in formal teaching certificate programs.

Networking opportunities. Each residency program has preceptors who will work with you as a coach and mentor, modeling clinical skills and providing valuable lessons in patient care, communication, and leadership. You may have a chance to work with different residents, depending on the size of the

continued on page 4

Sidebar 1-1. Benefits of Completing a Residency, *continued*

residency, and to interact with past program participants. You may be able to build relationships with physicians, other health care professionals, and academicians—relationships that open doors and help you with future career planning. You also can network at regional residency conferences and professional meetings.

Development of leadership skills. As a resident, you may serve on committees in your institution or take on leadership roles in the department or service. You will get to work on a research project and will likely be exposed to other project management opportunities throughout the year. You also may see how pharmacy is practiced in different parts of the country and in different settings, which exposes you to new ideas and different ways of thinking and helps you craft your personal practice style.

---

and many responsibilities to juggle at one time. I had strong mentors and graduate advisors to help guide my path, but they also allowed me freedom to explore different pharmacy and research opportunities. In addition, my residency helped me begin to develop my teaching skills.

Along the way, I ran into a few surprises—such as learning that I enjoyed internal medicine in a hospital setting. Before starting my residency, I thought I would definitely become an ambulatory care pharmacist. I also discovered that I liked working on research projects—and I don't mean the stuff I did back in chemistry lab, which is what the word "research" used to conjure up for me. I found it utterly absorbing to work on research projects that seek to answer clinical questions.

The long hours, hard work, and lack of sleep were worth it, because I'm now a clinical assistant professor at Purdue University with a practice site at a county hospital as an internal medicine specialist. I'm also a member of a global health team in the Purdue Kenya Program, which focuses on providing and expanding clinical pharmacy services in Western Kenya. I feel fortunate to be able to care for patients in both the United States and abroad, to educate students and residents, and to conduct research to help improve patient care. Without completing a residency program, I don't think I'd have the skills to be where I am—and I doubt if my job would be as professionally rewarding as the one I have.

Residency Program Overview

As defined by ASHP, the accrediting body for all accredited pharmacy residencies, a residency is "an organized, directed, postgraduate training program in a specific area of pharmacy practice."[3] It focuses on helping you develop the knowledge, attitudes, and skills to become a competent practitioner responsible for managing medication-use systems and accountable for optimal drug therapy outcomes. Residency programs are offered in many settings, including health systems, community pharmacies, long-term-care facilities, and managed care organizations.

> Residency training gives you extensive, hands-on experience in working with patients.

Residency training is primarily divided into two postgraduate years. PGY1 is more generalized, exposing you to a broad range of clinical scenarios and disease states. PGY2 programs allow you to specialize in an advanced area of pharmacy practice and increase the depth of knowledge, skills, and abilities you acquired during the PGY1 year. Before you can take part in a PGY2 residency, you must complete a PGY1 program. PGY2 programs are usually separate from PGY1 programs and require their own application and interview process. Some PGY1 programs are designed to be two years and participants in these programs sign a two-year contract with the site.

Postgraduate Year One (PGY1)

PGY1 residency programs provide a general pharmacy experience in hospitals and health systems, community practices, or managed care environments. ASHP has set standards and desired outcomes for these residency programs, which differ slightly based on the setting (see Tables 1-1 and 1-2).[4]

Hospital or Health-System PGY1 Programs

ASHP has developed standards for accrediting residency programs to ensure that residents receive structured training with direct supervision in a variety of practice settings. During a PGY1 residency you gain experience managing acutely ill and ambulatory care patients and you get

Table 1-1 | **Required Educational Outcomes for PGY1 Residency Programs**

PGY1 Pharmacy Residency Program	PGY1 Community Pharmacy Residency Program	PGY1 Managed Care Pharmacy Residency Program
		Outcome R1: Understand how to manage the drug distribution process for an organization's members.
Outcome R1: Manage and improve the medication-use process.	Outcome R1: Manage and improve the medication-use process.	Outcome R3: Ensure the safety and quality of the medication-use system.
Outcome R2: Provide evidence-based, patient-centered medication therapy management with interdisciplinary teams.	Outcome R2: Provide evidence-based, patient-centered care and collaborate with other health care professionals to optimize patient care.	Outcome R2: Design and implement clinical programs to enhance the efficacy of patient care.
Outcome R3: Exercise leadership and practice management skills.	Outcome R3: Exercise leadership and practice management skills.	Outcome R6: Exercise leadership and practice management skills.
Outcome R4: Demonstrate project management skills.	Outcome R4: Demonstrate project management skills.	Outcome R7: Demonstrate project management skills.
Outcome R5: Provide medications and practice-related education and training.	Outcome R5: Provide medication and practice-related information, education, and/or training.	Outcome R4: Provide medication and practice-related information, education, and/or training.
		Outcome R5: Collaborate with plan sponsors to design effective benefit structures to service a specific population's needs.
Outcome R6: Utilize medical informatics.	Outcome R6: Utilize medical informatics.	

Source: Adapted from American Society of Health-System Pharmacists. Required and elective educational outcomes, goals, objectives, and instructional objectives for postgraduate year one (PGY1) pharmacy residency programs, 2nd edition—effective July 2008. Available at: http://www.ashp.org/DocLibrary/Accreditation/Regulations-Standards/RTPPGY1GoalsObjectives. aspx. Accessed May 20, 2012.

Table 1-2 | **Elective Educational Outcomes for PGY1 Residency Programs**

PGY1 Pharmacy Residency Program	PGY1 Community Pharmacy Residency Program	PGY1 Managed Care Pharmacy Residency Program
	Outcome E1: Provide public health programs for health improvement, wellness, and disease prevention to the community.	
		Outcome E1: Added knowledge and skills to manage the drug distribution process for the organization's members.
Outcome E1: Conduct pharmacy practice research.	Outcome E3: Conduct pharmacy practice research.	Outcome E7: Conduct pharmacy practice research.
Outcome E2: Exercise added leadership and practice management skills.	Outcome E4: Exercise additional leadership and practice management skills.	Outcome E4: Exercise added leadership and practice management skills.
		Outcome E2: Provide evidence-based, patient-centered medication therapy management with interdisciplinary teams.
Outcome E3: Demonstrate knowledge and skills particular to generalist practice in the home care practice environment.	Outcome E9: Demonstrate knowledge and skills particular to generalist practice in the home care practice environment.	
		Outcome E3: Added knowledge and skills to provide medications and practice-related information, education, and/or training.
Outcome E4: Demonstrate knowledge and skills particular to generalist practice in the managed care practice environment.	Outcome E5: Demonstrate knowledge and skills for successful community practice interface with the managed care or self-insured employer environment.	

continued on page 8

Table 1-2 | **Elective Educational Outcomes for PGY1 Residency Programs,** *continued*

Outcome E5: Participate in the management of medical emergencies.	Outcome E2: Participate in planning for and/or management of medical and public health emergencies.	
		Outcome E5: Participate in the process by which managed care organizations contract with pharmaceutical manufacturers.
Outcome E6: Provide drug information to healthcare professionals and/or the public.		
		Outcome E6: Conduct outcomes-based research.
Outcome E7: Demonstrate additional competencies that contribute to working successfully in the health-care environment.		Outcome E9: Demonstrate additional competencies that contribute to working successfully in the health-care environment.
	Outcome E6: Demonstrate skills required to function in an academic setting.	
	Outcome E7: Create a community pharmacy drug information library.	
	Outcome E8: Participate in the organization's formulary management processes.	
		Outcome E8: Participate in the management of business continuity.

Source: Adapted from American Society of Health-System Pharmacists. Required and elective educational outcomes, goals, objectives, and instructional objectives for postgraduate year one (PGY1) pharmacy residency programs, 2nd edition—effective July 2008. Available at: http://www.ashp.org/DocLibrary/Accreditation/Regulations-Standards/RTPPGY1GoalsObjectives. aspx. Accessed May 20, 2012.

exposure to many disease states and pharmacotherapy issues. You rotate through different areas for a well-rounded learning experience, committing no more than a third of the year to any one specialty area, such as oncology or pediatrics.[4] For most rotation experiences, you work with a variety of preceptors, but this may not be true if you are at a small program or if one pharmacist covers several teams. You also get the opportunity to learn about drug information, drug-policy development, pharmacy administration, or practice management during rotations or longitudinal experiences throughout the entire residency year.

To learn about practice management, you are expected to function as a staff or clinical pharmacist within the department. Understanding an institution's distribution process gives you a good grasp of the importance of drug dosing, preparation, and delivery and how they relate to optimal clinical pharmacy decisions. The type of activities required of you and the time you must spend in the operational pharmacy (staffing) component of programs varies among institutions. Some options include:

- Working weekend shifts, such as every third weekend.

- Working one weekend evening per week.

- Being on call for designated periods each month.

  ○ Providing 24-hour clinical in-house coverage, which may require an overnight stay at the hospital.

  ○ Providing 24-hour coverage with availability via a pager, which requires accessibility via pager but no overnight stay at the hospital.

  ○ Being available for on-call clinical activities that may include code participation, pharmacokinetic assessments, antibiotic stewardship activities, nutrition support, and drug information services.

If you spend dedicated time on individual rotations or learning experiences in addition to carrying out the operational pharmacy component, you must comply with the Pharmacy Specific Duty Hours Requirements for the ASHP Accreditation Standards for Pharmacy Residencies, which are essentially your scheduled clinical and academic duties.[5] Such duties include any activity that can meet a residency standard (health fairs, staffing, rotations, teaching, and committee meetings). Each resident is not allowed to work more than 80 hours per week.

PGY1 residency programs in health systems differ based on the following:

- The overall health system, such as community hospital, academic medical center, or Veterans Affairs (VA) medical centers.

- The services the hospital or health system provides.

- The facility's affiliation with a college of pharmacy.

Table 1-3 lists some characteristics and differences in PGY1 residencies according to type of setting. Academic medical centers or large health systems tend to have more specialized patients and perform more interprofessional rounds because they have affiliations with schools of medicine, nursing, or pharmacy, as compared with community hospital settings. Community hospital residencies may have fewer residents, which can allow for more individualized training and learning opportunities that may not happen in larger institutions. If the residency is in a government institution, you can get experience in collaborative practice models and patient-centered medical home (PCMH) models. The VA model for PCMH is called a Patient Aligned Care Team. Electronic medical record systems and other technologies are integrated throughout national systems, such as the VA, whereas in local health-systems providers do not usually have access to patient records outside of their network.

Programs affiliated with a school or college of pharmacy tend to offer formalized teaching instruction, many teaching opportunities, and even teaching certificate programs, which can be important if you plan to seek an academic position when you complete your residency. Finally, some PGY1 programs also offer PGY2 programs at the same site, which is an advantage for those who want to pursue specialized training after the PGY1 year.

If you graduate from a PGY1 health-system residency and wish to pursue a PGY2 program, you can choose from a variety of practice settings, including academia. You can also move into a position as a full-time clinical pharmacy specialist, clinical coordinator, or clinical faculty member. Or you might go for a hybrid position with a mix of traditional dispensing roles and patient care activities.

Table 1-3 | Differences in PGY1 Health-System Residencies

	Academic Medical Centers or Large Health Systems	VA Medical Centers	Community Hospitals or Smaller Health Systems
Rounding	Daily rounds and collaboration with large interprofessional teams	Daily rounds and collaboration with interprofessional teams	May have less formalized daily rounds with more independent monitoring
Patient Population	May involve some specialized patient populations such as pediatrics, transplant, oncology, etc., in addition to general medicine and trauma patients	U.S. armed service veterans; large ambulatory care programs in a variety of disciplines; less acute care	Typically involves a generalized patient population in the areas of internal medicine, cardiology, common infectious diseases, etc.
Technology	Is usually integrated throughout entire system	A nationwide computer system	Is usually present but may not yet be integrated into entire system
Size of Residency Program	Typically a larger number of residents, which brings the potential to expand networking opportunities and collaborate on activities and projects; may have larger variety of preceptors and less flexibility with rotation schedule	Often small to medium programs	Often smaller numbers of residents, which brings the potential for more flexibility of rotations and learning opportunities, individualized training, and consistent feedback
Teaching Opportunities	Depending on affiliations with colleges or schools of pharmacy, it's common to have didactic teaching opportunities, a teaching certificate program, and precepting opportunities	Usually has precepting opportunities, may have a teaching certificate program, may be affiliated with colleges or schools of pharmacy	Usually has precepting opportunities and may have a teaching certificate program
Additional Training	Common to have PGY2 programs available at same site	Common to have PGY2 programs available at same site	May have PGY2 programs available at same site

Community Practice PGY1 Programs

The American Pharmacists Association established Community Pharmacy Residency Programs (CPRPs) in 1986 and partnered with ASHP to develop accreditation standards for CPRPs.[6] Practice training sites include chain, independent, supermarket, and health-system pharmacies. Community pharmacy residencies give you the opportunity to develop new patient care programs and work to change the community pharmacy setting. Specifically, you will:

- Provide evidence-based, patient-centered care in collaboration with other health care professionals.

- Focus on public health programs for wellness and disease prevention.

- Learn how to develop innovative pharmacy services to lead the community pharmacy profession into a more focused patient care arena.

Although you receive structured training, it is often longitudinal, in which you achieve objectives and have your learning assessed over a longer period of time than in hospital or health-system residencies. You typically have a primary preceptor for the entire residency year. In addition, you may take part in individual rotations for electives, specialty clinics, or pharmacy administration—a component of the residency program in which you devote time to business plan composition, new service development and implementation, marketing, and technology.

Like some health-system PGY1 programs, many community pharmacy residencies are affiliated with colleges and schools of pharmacy, which can give you opportunities to teach, get formalized teaching instruction, and take part in teaching certificate programs. In contrast to health-system PGY1 programs, community pharmacy residencies have an expectation that a resident will learn how to develop, implement, and evaluate a new or existing patient care service.[6]

If you graduate from a PGY1 CPRP, you may complete PGY2 programs or fellowships in various settings, including community pharmacy practice or academia, or you may accept a position as pharmacy owner, clinical coordinator or manager, clinical faculty member, or full-time clinical specialist in patient care activities. You may also elect a hybrid position that mixes traditional dispensing roles and patient care activities.

Managed Care PGY1 Programs

In managed care pharmacy, an expanding area of the health care field, efforts are made to balance cost efficiency with quality patient care while coordinating medical services and maintaining the best possible patient outcomes. The Academy of Managed Care Pharmacy worked with ASHP to design the standards used to accredit managed care residency programs,[7] which commonly occur within pharmacy benefit manager organizations, health maintenance organizations (HMOs), or health plans.

Managed care PGY1 pharmacy residencies give you experience in prescription benefits management, prior authorizations, drug utilization reviews, outcomes research, and specialty medication therapy management. You learn about resource utilization, preventive care benefit services, and disease state management programs through structured training in all of these areas. As in community pharmacy programs, the training is often longitudinal, so you achieve objectives and are assessed based on activities that span the entire residency as opposed to being assessed based on each monthly rotation completed.

In managed care residencies, you typically have few to no "staffing" requirements and you get less direct face-to-face interaction with patients than in other residency settings. Even so, you still participate in patient-centered care by managing cases, reviewing medication histories, and following up on recommendations.

If you graduate from a PGY1 managed care residency, you are likely to obtain positions with HMOs, pharmaceutical companies, medication therapy management vendors, consulting firms, drug information centers, or the VA health care system. You will probably start as a clinical managed care staff pharmacist, and then you may move into managerial and directorship roles.

Postgraduate Year Two (PGY2)

PGY2 residency programs train the resident in a designated specialty area. Unlike PGY1 programs, PGY2 programs are not classified as being in a hospital/health system, community, or managed care setting; they can be in a variety of areas within pharmacy. As you can see in Table 1-4, many options are available for a second, more advanced year of residency

Table 1-4 | Options for PGY2 Residencies

- Ambulatory Care Pharmacy
- Cardiology Pharmacy
- Critical Care Pharmacy
- Drug Information
- Emergency Medicine
- Geriatrics Pharmacy
- Health-System Pharmacy Administration
- Infectious Disease Pharmacy
- Informatics
- Internal Medicine Pharmacy
- Medication-Use Safety
- Nuclear Medicine Pharmacy
- Nutrition Support Pharmacy
- Oncology Pharmacy
- Pain Management and Palliative Care
- Pediatrics Pharmacy
- Pharmacotherapy
- Pharmacy Residency Training in an Advanced Area of Practice*
- Psychiatric Pharmacy
- Solid Organ Transplant Pharmacy

*Requires the development of outcomes, goals, and objectives.

Source: American Society of Health-System Pharmacists. Residency accreditation. http://www.ashp.org/menu/Accreditation/ResidencyAccreditation.aspx. Accessed May 20, 2012.

training. Table 1-4 is not an exhaustive list, but it does give an idea of accredited programs recognized by ASHP at the time this book went to press. Some PGY2 programs may take longer than a year to complete, especially if they are offered in combination with a master's degree, fellowship, or other type of training program. Similar to PGY1 programs, accredited PGY2 programs include both required and elective components, which are individualized for each specialty area.[8] But in contrast to the approach in many PGY1 programs, PGY2 programs may have residents work with only a few preceptors throughout the year. Completing PGY2 programs can prepare you for specialized clinical positions, research, academia, or leadership roles.

Nontraditional Programs

Nontraditional programs, which are designed for pharmacists already in practice, are becoming more common as the need grows for health systems to expand pharmacy services within their institutions. You usually complete the residency requirements over two to three years, depending on the site, but the program's goals and objectives must follow ASHP standards to maintain accreditation. If you're a nontraditional resident, you continue to serve as a staff or clinical pharmacist at your institution, and your residency rotations are scheduled around your service commitments.

To apply for some of these programs, you may have to be an employee of the institution for a certain period before the application process, and you may have to agree to a certain length of service after the residency is complete. Advantages that pharmacists gain from taking part in such programs include:

- Completing a residency program while maintaining employment and a full pharmacist salary.

I had not anticipated working in the hospital setting after pharmacy school, so I had focused on other skills during my last couple years of school and during rotations. After realizing I was not stimulated by retail pharmacy, I found a job working in a hospital as a staff pharmacist. However, I did not feel satisfied with how much I knew. I wanted to dig deeper into disease state management skills I could utilize in the hospital setting. So I sought a residency to help grow my knowledge base and find an area to specialize in.

—Eve McMichael

- Balancing residency training with family commitments.

- Receiving advanced training from a structured practice experience.

Benefits to the site may include:

- Having an advanced staff development program.

- Allowing for the potential expansion of clinical services.

- Increasing the likelihood of employee retention.

Accredited versus Nonaccredited Programs

Residency programs can be either accredited or nonaccredited. ASHP, which first started accrediting pharmacy residencies in 1962, is the only accrediting body for pharmacy residencies. To become accredited, an institution or site must demonstrate compliance with established standards of practice and offer a residency program that meets the requirements of training. Accredited programs undergo an on-site peer-review survey every six years. Survey teams comprise residency directors, preceptors, and other pharmacists knowledgeable about the residency process. Additionally, programs are required to submit written materials about the program at least every three years to maintain their accreditation in good standing.

The peer-review process ensures that accredited programs have excellent practice environments and that they achieve all requirements for the site, preceptors, and residency director. To complete accredited programs, residents must demonstrate proficiency in a set of defined outcomes and goals. The accreditation process helps ensure consistency among programs regardless of practice setting or physical location.

For various reasons, not all residencies seek accreditation status, such as having a unique program that does not fit a predetermined classification and set of standards. Some programs are not accredited simply because it is their first year of existence and, although they have started the accreditation process, they are not eligible to earn accreditation until their first resident has graduated from the program. If a program that interests you is not accredited, it is important to assess why not and consider the reasons in your decision-making process. To be part of the ASHP Resident Matching Program (the Match), which places applicants into pharmacy residency training positions in the United States, a residency must be accredited or must have initiated the process. (For further information on the Match, see Chapter 8.)

Fellowship Programs

A fellowship is an individualized postgraduate training program that is more research focused and less clinically oriented than a residency program. Programs are usually affiliated with a college or school of pharmacy, an academic health center, or the pharmaceutical industry (see Chapter 9). The purpose of fellowship programs is to develop independent and collaborative researchers.

If you pursue a fellowship, you build competency in the scientific research process, including how to design studies, obtain grants, collect, analyze, and interpret data, present research and findings, and submit manuscripts for publication. Before you start your program, you are expected to have practice skills relevant to the fellowship area—skills that you can acquire through previous practice or residency experience.[9] Fellowships generally take a minimum of two years to complete, but a few one-year programs are available, as well.

Graduate Degree Programs

The United States has many graduate degree programs, and each has different characteristics, including duration, content, requirements for candidates, program requirements for coursework and research, and so on. Pharmacy graduates who pursue master's degrees often choose science, public health, health care administration, or business administration. Common doctorate programs pharmacy graduates seek out include education (EdD), doctorate of public health, and doctorate of social and administrative pharmacy.

You can earn some advanced degrees in conjunction with doctor of pharmacy (PharmD) programs, residencies, and fellowship programs. Although it's beyond the scope of this book to discuss each type of program in detail, you can find more information on the websites of pharmacy colleges and schools, as well as on professional websites such as the ACCP directory of residencies, fellowships, and graduate programs and the ASHP residency directory site.

Conclusion

Residency programs are often the first step in making the transition from PharmD curriculums to clinical practice in health systems, community settings, or managed care. Participation in residency programs brings you both tangible and intangible benefits, such as advanced knowledge, solid skills, valuable contacts, in-depth exposure to new practice areas, and enhanced confidence in your clinical and leadership abilities.

I decided to pursue a residency after I'd been practicing in the community retail setting for three years. During my third year as a staff pharmacist at Kroger Pharmacy, I discovered the combined program offered by Duke and GlaxoSmithKline and thought it sounded like a perfect fit for what I was looking for.

I received many raised eyebrows when I told other pharmacists, residents, and students that I wanted to go back for a residency. My advice to anyone out there is that if you are motivated and passionate about specialization, it is never too late to pursue residency training. Leaving my position in community practice was not a difficult decision because I was excited and motivated to begin my new career path.

—Megan Zolman

References

1. Murphy JE, Nappi JM, Bosso JA, et al. American College of Clinical Pharmacy's vision of the future: postgraduate pharmacy residency training as a prerequisite for direct patient care practice. Pharmacotherapy. 2006;26:722–33.

2. American Society of Health-System Pharmacists. Professional policies approved by the 2007 ASHP House of Delegates. Am J Health Syst Pharm. 2007;64:e68–e71.

3. American Society of Health-System Pharmacists. General information for residencies. Available at: http://www.ashp.org/menu/Residents/GeneralInfo/FAQs.aspx#1. Accessed May 20, 2012.

4. American Society of Health-System Pharmacists. ASHP accreditation standard for postgraduate year one (PGY1) pharmacy residency programs. Available at: http://www.ashp.org/DocLibrary/Accreditation/ASD-PGY1-Standard.aspx. Accessed May 20, 2012.

5. American Society of Health-System Pharmacists. Pharmacy specific duty hours requirements for the ASHP accreditation standards for pharmacy residencies. Available at: http://www.ashp.org/DocLibrary/Accreditation/ASD-PGY1-Standard.aspx. Accessed May 20, 2012.

6. American Society of Health-System Pharmacists. Accreditation standard for postgraduate year one (PGY1) community pharmacy residency programs. Available at: http://www.ashp.org/DocLibrary/Accreditation/ASD-PGY1-Community-Standard.aspx. Accessed May 20, 2012.

7. American Society of Health-System Pharmacists. Accreditation standard for postgraduate year one (PGY1) managed care pharmacy residency programs. Available at: http://www.ashp.org/DocLibrary/Accreditation/ ASD-Managed-Care-Standard.aspx. Accessed May 20, 2012.

8. American Society of Health-System Pharmacists. Residency accreditation-PGY2 outcomes, goals, and objectives. Available at: http://www.ashp.org/menu/Accreditation/ResidencyAccreditation.aspx. Accessed May 20, 2012.

9. American College of Clinical Pharmacy. Guidelines for clinical research fellowship training programs. Available at: http://www.accp.com/resandfel/guidelines.aspx. Accessed May 20, 2012.

Chapter 2

Setting the Foundation for a Residency Position

By Monica L. Miller and Deanna Kania

Competition for residency positions increases every year—with the number of applicants growing faster than the slots available. Statistics are hard to pin down, because they keep changing, but applicants have roughly a 60% chance of being accepted into an accredited residency. To increase their odds, candidates want answers to two key questions:

- What are residency programs looking for?

- What can I do to set myself apart?

With so many students vying for limited positions, it's imperative to work on putting your very best foot forward. This chapter identifies characteristics that residency directors are looking for in candidates and outlines steps you can take during pharmacy school to set a strong foundation for participation in a residency program.

I recognized early that leadership and organizational involvement were important to me. I began my involvement with the American Society of Health-System Pharmacists as a student serving on the National Policy Council on Pharmacy Practice, and now ASHP is part of my day-to-day career, benefiting me in countless ways, including constant exchanges of advice, best practices, and information about hot professional issues.

—John Hertig

Desirable Characteristics of Residents

Do you have what it takes to be accepted into a residency program? Programs look for many different qualities, but overall they want candidates who are well-rounded and have strong personal characteristics, including the ability to communicate well with patients, fit into a team, and work effectively in professional settings. Table 2-1, compiled from unpublished surveys of residency program directors, lists characteristics that directors want candidates to possess. You hone these attributes during pharmacy school and by participating in extracurricular activities. Then, you demonstrate that you have them by including relevant information in your curriculum vitae (discussed in Chapter 4) and by promoting yourself effectively during the interview process (discussed in Chapter 7).

Table 2-1 | Desirable Personal Characteristics of Residents

- Self-motivated
- Confident (but not arrogant)
- Good time-management skills
- Positive attitude
- Team player
- Independent
- Effective leadership skills
- Well-developed communication skills
- Professional
- Mature

Setting a Strong Foundation

In addition to looking for applicants who possess the personal characteristics in Table 2-1, residency programs want you to be dedicated to the profession and to have had broad experiences during pharmacy school. They also like you to stand out from the crowd rather than doing only what's "typical." Table 2-2 suggests ways to build a solid foundation for acceptance into a residency. This chapter covers each of these topics in more detail.

Table 2-2 | **Ways to Set a Strong Foundation for Residency Acceptance**

- Maintain a solid grade point average (GPA).
- Demonstrate professional curiosity.
- Participate in professional organizations and their associated activities.
- Develop leadership skills.
- Participate in research projects with faculty members.
- Get involved in community service activities.
- Develop positive relationships with faculty, pharmacists, and fellow students.
- Know who you want to be as a pharmacist.

Maintain a Solid GPA

Maintaining a GPA above 3.0 is important if you plan to seek a residency because it demonstrates a strong base of learning and the motivation to do well in school. A solid knowledge base gives you a foundation for developing clinical skills. If you don't get the most you can out of your core pharmacy classes, how will you be equipped to care for patients—whether you plan to pursue a residency or not?

Even if you're seeking a residency that doesn't focus on patient care, a good GPA is required because it shows your competency in the materials presented during pharmacy school. If you actively participate in outside activities at the same time you maintain good grades, it suggests you have well-developed time-management skills, which are important for success in a residency. If your pharmacy program doesn't use the GPA system, make sure you receive a "Pass" in each class or module.

Your GPA is included on your pharmacy school transcript, which most residencies require you to submit as part of the application packet. Residency programs use the GPA and other transcript information, such as performance in specific classes and GPA in pharmacy courses, to help evaluate knowledge base before deciding whether to meet a residency candidate.

Each residency program utilizes the GPA differently when assessing applications. Some have a specific GPA cutoff, which is usually outlined in the application requirements. Others accept a GPA range—with the higher GPAs given higher value on their selection rubic. When reviewing transcripts, programs may also look at your performance in therapeutics and pharmacology classes to assess your clinical knowledge base.

Keep in mind that a high GPA, even a 4.0, doesn't guarantee you'll get a residency position. Having a low GPA, however, can hurt your application. Even so, grades alone do not make a strong residency candidate. If you do not have a high GPA, see Chapter 7 for helpful interviewing tips related to GPA.

Demonstrate Professional Curiosity

Programs want to know you are interested in the profession of pharmacy as a lifelong passion and not simply a "9 to 5" job opportunity. This really means that studying isn't everything; you also need to participate in professional activities for a well-rounded understanding of the profession.

Actively learning about the profession allows you to speak about it intelligently, get details about the areas you're interested in, and clearly identify the role of a pharmacist in a variety of settings. You'll also be able to discuss challenges and opportunities you believe lie ahead for the profession. Being able to clearly articulate why you're interested in pharmacy, the specific areas you are drawn to, and the direction pharmacy is heading will show you've done your homework and will make you stand out in an interview.

Some specific ways you can demonstrate your passion for and curiosity about pharmacy include the following:

- Seek employment in various areas of pharmacy such as community and hospital pharmacy, long-term care, managed care, compounding, and others.

- Shadow pharmacists in a variety of practice settings for a full or half day. You can arrange shadowing experiences by asking professors and other pharmacy contacts about pharmacists they know who would be willing to have you observe them at work.

> Programs seek residents who view the profession of pharmacy as a lifelong passion and not simply a "9 to 5" job opportunity.

- Volunteer in different pharmacy practice settings.

- Participate in professional organizations by attending state, regional, and national meetings, joining committees, and getting involved in programs sponsored by these organizations.

- Develop professional relationships and contacts through the activities listed in the four bullets above.

- Ask people questions about their work, listen closely, and engage in good conversation skills. Share your aspirations and ask others how they have gotten to this spot in their career.

- Attend legislative days to advocate for the profession. Legislative days are often sponsored by state pharmacy organizations or schools and colleges of pharmacy and include such activities as speaking with lawmakers about policies or budget issues that affect pharmacy.

- Participate in health fairs and other professional service activities sponsored by your school or student organizations, which gives you a chance to talk with patients and develop patient care skills.

- Collaborate with faculty or other pharmacists on additional projects outside of normal coursework, such as doing research projects, working on a publication, helping out with a course, or getting involved in a project at the pharmacy where you work.

This is not an exhaustive list. You don't have to participate in all the activities mentioned here to be a competitive residency candidate—but it's important to commit yourself to several different ones. Pick activities you are genuinely interested in so you have fun while learning about the profession.

Join Professional Organizations

Participating in professional organizations is such a key to success that even though it's touched upon in the list above, it bears further emphasis. Among the many intangible benefits of belonging to professional groups is developing friendships with pharmacists and student pharmacists across the country—which is the essence of networking. Undoubtedly, these friends will help you in your career along the way. Schools offer students access to professional organizations at the school, state, and national levels through student chapters.

I (Monica) felt that my involvement in professional organizations was one of the best parts of pharmacy school. I am a naturally shy person who gets nervous talking in front of people, and sometimes I even struggle to make small talk. Today, most people who see me in action would never believe this. But my parents and sister, who have witnessed my shyness my whole life, know how far I have come.

I can honestly say that taking part in professional organizations during my student days at the Minnesota College of Pharmacy is what helped me break out of my shell. As a first-year student, I became involved in an alliance that represented all the national and state pharmacy organizations, and as a result I got to know peers and upperclassmen. Soon, with the encouragement of fellow students and mentors, I migrated into leadership roles. Eventually I became chapter president and ran for regional and national positions within APhA's Academy of Student Pharmacists.

Among the many things I took away from these experiences were how to work with a variety of people, find a common goal, start new projects, delegate work, and cheer on team members—skills I have used many times in my professional work environment and would never have learned in a classroom. I also gained knowledge about the profession, overcame my shyness, and made many good friends who remain in my life today for weekend socializing, shopping, holiday gatherings—and they serve as professional sounding boards and collaborators. Table 2-3 provides a list of benefits of taking part in professional organizations.

Table 2-3 | Benefits of Involvement in Professional Organizations

- Taking advantage of networking opportunities, which help you build contacts and friendships.
- Having opportunities for leadership positions that allow you to build skills for professional advancement.
- Developing professional communication skills.
- Learning about the profession from other members instead of relying on the textbook.
- Serving as an advocate for the profession.
- Getting exposed to different patient care learning opportunities.

Develop Leadership Skills

All student pharmacists seeking residency positions need leadership skills, which you can develop in a variety of ways. Forget the old saying that "leaders are born, not made." And don't subscribe to the misconception that only people in traditional leadership roles are leaders. Being a leader is more than a position title; it's about having a vision for the profession that you actively work toward. Below is a list of some obvious and not-so-obvious leadership activities.

- Lead a patient care activity.

- Work on a research project.

- Be a member of a college committee, such as a curriculum committee or class gift committee.

- Take part in a JRCOSTEP program through the Junior Commissioned Officer Student Training and Extern Program of the U.S. Public Health Service Commissioned Corps (http://usphs.gov/student/jrcostep.aspx).

- Participate in internships or advanced pharmacy practice experiences (APPEs) at state or national pharmacy associations.

I was highly involved in activities on the Purdue University Campus, but not so much at the pharmacy school itself, because I needed an escape. I took on leadership in Purdue's new student orientation, at my church, and as the crew chief for our Grand Prix team, which allowed me to spread my wings beyond the world of pharmacy.

— Ed Battjes

- Participate in internships or APPEs within the pharmaceutical industry. See Table 2-4 for examples of pharmaceutical companies that offer opportunities to students.

- Become a committee member for a student, state, or national organization.

- Get involved in teaching opportunities at your school.

- Participate in competitions through professional organizations. See Table 2-5 for a listing of competitions to consider.

- Work at a free clinic.

- Write an article for the college or school or pharmacy's newsletter, for a professional blog, or for a local newspaper or magazine.

This list could go on for pages, but it gives you an idea of creative ways you can exercise your leadership skills and apply your knowledge. Use it as a starting point to brainstorm about possibilities. Think about activities that allow you to work with a team and be in charge of some aspect of a project. For example, I (Monica) had a student whose "out of the box" leadership opportunity involved bicycling 3700 miles across the country with other riders in the Journey of Hope bicycle ride to raise money and awareness for people with disabilities.

Table 2-4 | **Examples of Pharmaceutical Companies Offering Student Learning Experiences**

Company	Website
Abbott Laboratories	www.abbott.com/careers/students/internship-programs/us.htm
Amgen	http://www.amgen.com/careers/campus.html
Eli Lilly & Co	http://lilly.com/careers/student-opportunities/Pages/internships.aspx
Genentech	www.gene.com/gene/careers/interns_coops.html
GlaxoSmithKline	http://us.gsk.com/html/career/career-summer.html
Johnson & Johnson	http://careers.jnj.com/Internship-co-op-programs
Merck	www.merck.com/careers/explore-careers/students-and-graduates/home.html
Novartis	www.us.novartis.com/careers/undergraduate-internship.shtml
Sanofi Pasteur	http://careers.sanofipasteur.us/index.cfm?fa=app.internships
Pfizer	http://pfizercareers.com/university-relations
Vertex Pharmaceuticals	http://vertex.sc.hodesdigital.com/universityRelations/internship

Table 2-5 | **Professional Competitions for Students**

Competition	Sponsoring Organization and Web Link	Description
Clinical Pharmacy Challenge	American College of Clinical Pharmacy www.accp.com/stunet/ compete/overview.aspx	Tests pharmacy knowledge of student teams comprised of third and final year professional students.
National Student Pharmacist P&T Competition	Academy of Managed Care Pharmacy (AMCP) www.amcp.org/fmcpPT	Gives student teams hands-on experience working with a formulary management challenge that could be faced by a pharmacy and therapeutics (P&T) committee.
National Patient Counseling Competition	American Pharmacists Association (APhA) www.pharmacist.com/ node/24041	Recognizes students who have skills for providing patient education about medications.
Clinical Pharmacy Challenge	American College of Clinical Pharmacy www.accp.com/stunet/ compete/overview.aspx	Tests pharmacy knowledge of student teams comprised of third and final year professional students.
Good Neighbor Pharmacy NCPA Pruitt-Schutte Student Business Plan Competition	National Community Pharmacists Association (NCPA) www.ncpanet.org/index. php/business-plan- competition	This team competition encourages student interest in independent community pharmacy; teams draft a business proposal for either purchasing an independent pharmacy or starting their own pharmacy.

You can also gain leadership experience in extracurricular activities that are not associated with pharmacy, such as organizing a food drive for your favorite charity or serving on the university's student council. Leadership in sports, coaching children's sports teams, campus organizations, work activities, and community groups such as the Alzheimer's Association, the Boys and Girls Club, or the Glee Club are meaningful as well. Such activities demonstrate that you can plan, take charge, think on your feet, manage your time, and see efforts through. They also show that you are well rounded, with personal interests outside of the classroom. Keep in mind the following tips:

- **Pick activities that truly interest you.** Do not get involved simply to put something on your curriculum vitae; look to enhance your skills and meet your professional goals.

- **Keep up your grades.** Do not overextend yourself and let your schoolwork suffer while you participate in outside activities. Maintaining good grades while you take part in professional and extracurricular activities shows that you can balance patient care and other residency responsibilities.

- **Become involved nationally as well as locally.** This helps you build a broader network across the country.

- **Be willing to try something new.** Step outside your comfort zone to grow in multiple dimensions and identify new interests.

Participate in Research

Doing a research project not only sets you apart, it also demonstrates professional curiosity and leadership. Like many students, you may associate research with large clinical trials or projects performed in laboratories, and therefore you think you can't participate. But pharmacists get involved in many different research projects involving clinical patient care, student education, health care economics, and other areas.

> Pharmacists get involved in many different research projects involving clinical patient care, student education, health care economics, and other areas.

Many pharmacy programs require students to complete a research project as a graduation requirement. If yours does, great, but if it doesn't, seek out a project anyway. It will be a good learning experience and may boost your strength as a residency candidate. During your residency interview, it's decidedly a plus to be able to talk about your research project. Examples I've come across recently include conducting a survey about a class, reviewing a disease state in a specific population, creating a new teaching tool, reviewing a clinical order set for a hospital, and working in a laboratory analyzing proteins. Projects can be completed in all areas of pharmacy, and there really are no restrictions on the types of projects you can complete. It's all about getting experience in asking questions and finding ways to obtain answers. Table 2-6 covers benefits of participating in research projects.

Table 2-6 | **Potential Benefits of Participating in Research Projects**

- Being mentored by, and developing a long-term relationship with, a faculty member.

- Writing a research article and possibly having it published, which gives you professional clout.

- Presenting a poster at a professional meeting, which allows you to network and to polish your presentation skills.

- Developing research skills that will come in useful later, during your residency project.

- Demonstrating your professional curiosity and your desire to explore the profession.

- Learning to manage multiple types of activities at once, including research and schoolwork.

- Developing grant-writing skills, which are useful in many areas of pharmacy and health care.

- Getting practice in writing an institutional review board submission, which is required in all residency projects.

Because most faculty members have to participate in research for promotion and tenure, you should have no problem finding a willing faculty partner. You can also work with pharmacists you meet at your introductory pharmacy practice experience (IPPE) and APPE sites who are involved in projects of their own.

When I (Monica) was a student, I worked on a research project that evaluated the literature published about interprofessional teams, which helped me learn how to properly conduct a literature review. It also cemented my professional relationship with an academic pharmacist who mentored me through the residency selection process. Now, as a professor, I mentor students on their own research projects—from an educational program about deworming medications, which was presented to children in Kenya, to a survey for identifying signs of reverse culture shock, which was given to students who went on an international APPE experience. Through such projects, students learn what it takes to complete research successfully and they develop greater confidence in themselves.

When deciding on a project, make sure you'll be able to finish it once you start. Table 2-7 provides a list of ways to ensure you successfully complete a research project.

Table 2-7 | Tips for Successful Research Projects

- Seek out a project early in your professional program.

- Ensure that you are pulling your weight on the project by sharing the workload, completing work on deadline, and communicating with team members.

- Stay in good communication with your faculty counterpart, including sending frequent email updates without being prompted.

- Seek out a project you are interested in rather than one you think will impress a residency director. Your heart must be in the work.

- Be flexible about timeline extensions (which may result from delays in institutional review board approval) and changes in other aspects of the project.

Participate in Community Service

Participating in community service activities shows that you are a well-rounded person with interests that are not related only to pharmacy. It also suggests that you have a solid sense of responsibility and a spirit of giving back—important in a service-related profession like pharmacy.

Community service activities can be anything from participating in a local charity, organizing a community or charity event, reading to patients at a children's hospital, or volunteering at a nursing home. Many schools incorporate service into curricula to expose students to the idea of giving back to the community. When I (Monica) was in school, I found it rewarding to get out of the classroom and connect with people in my community to help them understand their medicine or disease states. I've heard of student pharmacists developing a babysitting service for families with special-needs children—with care provided by people with proper medical training—and of students gathering medical supplies for communities in need internationally. There's no limit to the kinds of things you can do to help others.

Develop Positive Relationships

Developing positive working relationships with faculty members, preceptors, other pharmacists and fellow students will be a great benefit during your residency search. Faculty members will be able to write you favorable letters of recommendation detailing specific strengths, rather than generic letters. If you have a positive relationship with them, they will *want* to help you secure a residency and employment. And they'll say good things about you to their colleagues.

Likewise, your peers can help you by telling you about jobs or residency opportunities and sharing other helpful bits of information. They can support you (and you can support them) through the challenges of pharmacy school and you can commiserate with each other after a bad test or rotation experience. Those with whom you build strong relationships will become professional colleagues who can speak highly of you after graduation.

To prepare for a residency position, I studied a lot and got involved in professional organizations, such as APhA-ASP and our school's pharmacy student government. I helped with blood pressure screenings for fans at basketball games, educated people about the flu vaccine, shadowed pharmacists in various settings, and took part in other activities that allowed me to retain material rather than learning it for a test and then forgetting it.

— Colleen Teevan

Know What You Want

Only you can answer the question, "What do I want?" What sort of pharmacy career are you seeking and how do you want to be regarded in the profession? You may not know for sure now, but taking part in the activities and learning experiences described in this chapter will help you figure it out.

Of course, you don't have to do all these things to be considered for a residency. Pick and choose wisely and do your very best in each activity. At the same time, maintain good academic standing and interact with people outside of class. Residency programs will be evaluating you as a whole person.

Gaining Experience Later in Pharmacy School

Although it's best to become involved and build varied skills throughout pharmacy school, some of you may have gotten a late start because of family or work obligations. Even so, it's still possible for you to obtain a residency. Start now to network with pharmacists and take part in activities. Think creatively, ask for opportunities, and don't be afraid to take on new roles. Examples of worthwhile steps to take include the following:

- Get to know the preceptors for your IPPE and APPE experiences.

- Work on a research project and strive to have it presented at a meeting.

- Participate in community service activities and take on a leadership role.

- Seek leadership positions at your place of employment and at your school.

- Join professional organizations and be active by attending meetings, helping with projects, and joining committees.

- Volunteer to serve on panels during pharmacy school interview days.

- Become a liaison between student organizations and local counterparts.

- Write an article for a peer-reviewed publication.

Conclusion

Many of the characteristics that residency programs look for take time to develop, so you should start getting involved in activities as soon as possible. But it is never too late. Pharmacy school should never be all work and no play. Participate in professional and extracurricular activities not only to build your skills, but also to meet new people, form friendships, take a break from the books, and have fun.

Chapter 3

Researching Residency Programs

By Molly A. Mason, Monica L. Miller, and Deanna Kania

Researching residency programs may seem like a daunting task. There are so many programs, and they vary widely in the experiences they offer residents. How do you decide which programs might be a good fit for you?

First, knowing what you are looking for will help you narrow your residency search and target the programs you want to learn more about. From your experiences in pharmacy school; talking to family, friends and colleagues; and working with a mentor you probably already have ideas about what you want and don't want from a residency. To become even more focused, you should consider factors such as your career goals, the areas of pharmacy that are most interesting to you, and the range and types of experiences you'd like a residency to provide.

When I (Monica) began searching for a residency program, I felt very stressed because I thought I'd never be able to narrow down my selection from the hundreds of options. Plus I was looking at programs in states I was not from and places where I didn't know residency directors. I spent hours searching through residency directories offered by national pharmacy asso-

When searching for residency programs, I utilized the residency directory on the ASHP website to get information and generate a list of potential options. Unaccredited programs, such as those just starting, may not have information online, so for those programs I searched for contact information and got in touch with the program directors to obtain specifics.

—Ashley Crumby

ciations and looking at individual websites of pharmacy residencies, trying to match the information with my own criteria. I wanted a residency focused on ambulatory care, with teaching opportunities and a small residency class size, located somewhere outside of Minnesota. I found so many programs meeting my criteria that I needed to prune the list further—and soon I added more criteria: an MS program in conjunction with the residency and diverse experiences outside of ambulatory care.

I ended up being interested in about 20 different programs before I went to the Midyear Clinical Meeting of the American Society of Health-System Pharmacists, where I talked with residency program directors and past residents to clarify my choices. For more information about connecting with residency programs at meetings and showcases, see Chapter 5.

> Knowing what you are looking for will help you narrow your residency search and target the programs you want to learn more about.

Your Career Goals

As a first step in the residency search process, you'll want to think about the goals you have for your pharmacy career. Your goals are as individual as you are. You might want to work with an indigent population, making a difference in an impoverished area, while your colleague might be drawn to research opportunities.

To help you identify your goals, consider factors such as the skills you want to develop, the accomplishments you hope to achieve, your strengths, and what you might want to do after your residency program. For instance, one of my (Monica) career goals was to become a strong clinical pharmacist in either ambulatory care or internal medicine. I went into pharmacy school knowing that I wanted to be part of an interprofessional health care team, and keeping this in mind, I knew that community pharmacy residency programs were not where I needed to be, and I could also avoid looking at drug information, pharmacy administration, or association management programs. I wanted to develop my teaching skills, so it made sense to target residencies with a teaching certificate program. In addition, I wanted to work with an underserved population, so I looked for programs that would accommodate this goal.

Once you have identified a few of your goals, think about how each influences the type of residency you are seeking. Ask yourself, How could participating in a residency program help me achieve this goal? Having this information gives you a starting point for your search.

Next, consider the characteristics you desire in a program, both to further your goals and to explore the types of practices that most interest you.

What Are You Looking for in a Residency Program?

As you learn more about potential residency programs, you will see that you have many choices to ponder. Are you interested in working in a health system or a community setting? Does a large or small program appeal to you? What areas of pharmacy and which patient populations spark your interest? How do you choose from so many possibilities? Sidebar 3-1 contains a list of questions to help you identify what is important to you in a residency program. Working through these questions will help you become clearer about your preferences and will make your search more efficient and effective.

Sidebar 3-1. Questions to Focus Your Residency Search

The answers to these questions will help you determine what you are looking for in a residency program.

Areas of Interest

• Do you want to work in a hospital/health-system setting or a community setting?

• What type of patient care interests you?

  ○ Ambulatory care

  ○ Community pharmacy

  ○ Emergency medicine

  ○ Infectious disease

  ○ Cardiology

  ○ Oncology

continued on page 38

Sidebar 3-1. Questions to Focus Your Residency Search, *continued*

- ○ Internal medicine

- ○ Nutrition support

- ○ Pain management/palliative care

- ○ Transplant

- ○ Informatics

- ○ Pediatrics

- ○ Geriatrics

- ○ Drug Information

- ○ Psychiatry

- ○ Medication Safety

- ○ Other

- Are you interested in community pharmacy?

- Are you interested in managed care?

- Are you interested in pharmacy management?

- Would you like to get an additional advanced degree (MS, MPH, MHA)?

- Would you like to participate in a postgraduate year 2 (PGY2) program?

- With what population of patients do you enjoy working (underserved, geriatrics, etc.)?

Desired Program Setting

- Do you want to work at a teaching hospital?

- Would you be interested in working at a community hospital?

- Are you interested in community pharmacy?

- Do you prefer more ambulatory care experiences?

- Would you like to work within the Veterans Affaris system caring for veterans?

- Would you like a program with access to elective rotations in rural settings?

- Would you like to participate in an elective experience outside of the United States?

Sidebar 3-1, *continued*

Geographic Location

- Are you willing to relocate for your residency?

- What part of the country/world do you want to live in?

- Do you want to live in a big city or a small town?

- What are your extracurricular activities and where can you best pursue them?

- How far away are members of your support team, such as family and friends?

- What is the cost of living in the area in which you are interested?

Residency Class Size

- Would you like a large program or a small program?

  ○ Large: 10+ residents

  ○ Medium: 5–9 residents

  ○ Small: 1–4 residents

Teaching Opportunities

- Do you want to teach at some point?

- What type of teaching opportunities appeal to you?

- Do you want to participate in a teaching certificate program?

- Would you like to participate in didactic teaching?

- Would you like to be a preceptor?

- Would you like the opportunity to participate in course coordination?

Research Opportunities

- How involved would you like to be in research?

- Would you be interested in a formalized research program or fellowship?

- What type of research project appeals to you?

- Would you like a program that collaborates with affiliated academic institutions?

continued on page 40

Sidebar 3-1. Questions to Focus Your Residency Search, *continued*

College Affiliation

- Would you like to be affiliated with a college or school of pharmacy?

- Would you like to be affiliated with the college or school of pharmacy from which you received your degree?

Professional Organization Involvement

- Is it important for you to maintain involvement in professional organizations during your residency?

- In which organizations are you currently involved?

- If you are required to take vacation time to participate in professional meetings, how will this affect your membership?

PGY2 Residency Opportunities

- Do you want to be affiliated with a program that has many PGY2 residency options for you to select from after your first year?

- Are you willing to move for a PGY2 residency?

Other Questions

- What type of support system will you have during your residency?

- Would you like to participate in an on-call service as a resident?

- Do you have an interest in project management/development?

After you have answered these questions, develop a list of program characteristics that are important to you. You may also want to consider which items are priorities and those on which you may be willing to compromise. Examples of characteristics include the following:

- Larger residency class.

- Training certificate.

- Teaching hospital.

- Affiliation with a college of pharmacy.

- PGY2 in internal medicine.

- Paid travel to one meeting.

Though you may not identify a program that has every item you are searching for, probably a number of programs will seem to be good fits. You may decide to revisit the questions in Sidebar 3-1 periodically, especially during your final year of pharmacy school. Different rotation experiences during that year may cause you to rethink your answers. Also, review your list with a trusted mentor who may be able to recommend additional questions to ask yourself as you whittle your list of potential programs.

When to Start Searching

It is best to start searching for residency programs late in your third, or next to last, professional year or early in your fourth, or final, professional year. Sidebar 3-2 contains suggestions for timing each step of your residency search. You can also attend national, regional, or local meetings, as discussed in Chapter 5, to learn more about programs and future options.

Researching Residency Programs

There are many ways you can research residency programs. Often students begin their search on the Internet looking at online residency directories, and then they gather more information by networking, attending college-sponsored residency showcases, investigating institution-specific websites, and contacting programs directly.

Online Directories

Many professional pharmacy organizations maintain online directories of residency programs, which are accessible to the public at no cost and provide valuable information about opportunities for advanced training in clinical pharmacy practice and research. Organizations that offer directories with residency listings include:

- American College of Clinical Pharmacy (ACCP)

- Academy of Managed Care Pharmacy (AMCP)

- American Pharmacists Association (APhA)

- American Society of Health-System Pharmacists (ASHP)

- Indian Health Service (IHS)

For more information about these organizations' directories, see Table 3-1.

Sidebar 3-2. Timeline for Your Residency Search

Below are suggestions for when to complete the steps in your residency search.

- 1st–3rd professional year
  - Attend state, regional, and national meetings
  - Evaluate clinical interests and geographic interests or limitations
- 4th professional year
  - May/June
    - Re-evaluate clinical interests and geographic interests or limitations
    - Begin searching online directories
    - Compile a list of potential programs
    - Discuss plans with mentors
    - Ask graduates from your school about different options
  - August
    - Prioritize future career goals
    - Conduct searches on programs that seem to be good fits for you
    - Create a list of programs
    - Contact programs you are interested in to get more information
  - September–December
    - Attend regional and national residency showcases
    - Focus your list of programs
    - Submit applications

Table 3-1 | **Residency Directories of Professional Pharmacy Associations**

Directory Owner	Web Link to Online Directory	Program Information Included	Directory Is Especially Useful for Learning About...
American College of Clinical Pharmacy	https://www.accp.com/resandfel	• Program Type • Type of Residency • Program Institution • Available Positions • Program Length • Accreditation Type	• Accredited and nonaccredited residencies • Traditional research fellowships • Graduate school programs
Academy of Managed Care Pharmacy	www.amcp.org/Residencies	• Company Name • Residency/Program Type • Accreditation Status • Program Length • Number of Available Positions • College of Pharmacy Affiliation • Application Deadline • On-site Interview Requirement • Education/Specials Application Requirement • Benefits • Special Program Features	• Accredited and nonaccredited managed care residencies • Industry fellowships
American Pharmacists Association	www.pharmacist.com/residency	• Program Information • Affiliated Site Addresses • Selection Criteria • Application Deadline • Program Description • Benefits • National Matching Service (NMS) Number	• PGY1 programs based in community pharmacy practice
American Society of Health-System Pharmacists	www.ashp.org/menu/Accreditation/ResidencyDirectory.aspx	• NMS Code • Accreditation Status • Residency Type • Director of Pharmacy • Program Duration • Number of Available Positions • Application Deadline • Interview Requirements • Residency Special Features • Fringe Benefits • Special Requirements for Acceptance • Institution Type • Institution Demographics	• Accredited PGY1 programs • Accredited PGY2 programs

continued on page 44

Table 3-1 | Residency Directories of Professional Pharmacy Associations, *continued*

Indian Health Service	www.ihs.gov/ medicalprograms/ pharmacy/ resident/	• Location • Training Site Type • Accreditation Status • Rotation Opportunities • Pharmacy Director name and contact • Facility Description • Special Features	• IHS COSTEP program (Commissioned Officer Student Training and Extern Program) • IHS residency programs

Networking

Networking is one of the best ways to establish a connection within residency programs. Having a personal contact can open doors to opportunities that may not be posted on an online directory and give you access to information that's not on a program's website. Once you know that you want to pursue residency training, you can begin networking with your school's faculty members, your mentors, or other pharmacists you may know. If one of them has a position you're interested in, ask about his or her career path. You may want to ask to shadow him or her to observe a typical day and get a better idea of what the position involves.

You can also discuss residency training with clinical pharmacy specialists, your professional colleagues, and current residents at programs that interest you. Experienced people in the field can provide valuable "insider" information and advice.

College-Sponsored Showcases

Many colleges around the country offer showcases for pharmacy residency programs within a particular region. Attending these showcases allows you to browse among the programs and chat face-to-face with their representatives. Programs will have some sort of display, packets of information providing specific details, and personnel on site to answer questions. These events are much smaller than a national residency showcase, such as the one held at the ASHP Midyear Clinical Meeting. For more information on residency showcases, see Chapter 5.

Your pharmacy school will have information about upcoming showcases in your area and across the country. Typically they announce this information on their website and in student newsletters.

Institution-Specific Websites

Browsing a residency program's website is a great way to gain more detail than is offered on the residency directory websites. You may find a list of preceptors, their required and elective rotations, and the current and past residents' names. You will also be able to learn more about the individual practice site, such as hospital size, number of affiliated clinics, and associated training programs for other health care providers.

Contacting Programs Directly

After you identify programs that interest you, you may have specific questions about information that is not readily available on a website or in a directory. You may want to speak to someone directly to get a "feel" for the program. The first point of contact is usually the residency director. His or her email address will be listed in the residency directory and on the program's website.

When you contact the director for more information, ask questions that the website does not readily answer. (You don't want to seem like you didn't bother to do a little research on the program first.) You can also ask to be put into contact with residents, if you have specific questions for them. When you contact programs directly, draft professional emails, ask questions that allow you to delve further than what is presented on the website, and remember that, in essence, you're starting an interview process. Your email will play a big part in the first impression formed by the person with whom you correspond. Figure 3-1 is a sample email that demonstrates principles of clear, direct, professional writing.

When searching for my PGY1 residency, I began by deciding what experiences were important to me in a residency program. Then I pinpointed where I was willing to live. Using the ASHP residency directory, I took detailed notes on every residency within the states I was willing to move to, and if they did not contain every one of my requirements, I struck them off my list. On my final list, I ranked the programs and emailed the top 10 or 15 to get my name out there and gather more information from residency directors and residents. After talking with them, I dropped any that did not feel like a good fit and decided which programs to apply to.

—Isabel Hagedorn

Figure 3-1 | **Sample Email for Contacting Residency Programs**

Hello, Dr./Ms./Mr._____,
My name is Monica Miller and I am a fourth-year PharmD student from the University. I have reviewed your ASHP residency listing and am very interested in applying for your PGY1 residency position.

When I reviewed your website, I read that you have a progressive pharmacy department. I was wondering if you could tell me more about the staff pharmacist's role and how this position interacts with your clinical pharmacists. Also, could you tell me what type of research projects your residents have completed in the past?

I know that you are busy and I appreciate your taking the time to answer my questions.

Sincerely,

Monica Miller
PharmD Candidate – The University College of Pharmacy

Tracking Your Search

During the search process, keep good records of the programs you are investigating. You may even want to use a chart or table to track information and compare program offerings. You could include fields for such information as the program website, residency director contact information, start date, stipend or salary, and other details. During my residency search, I (Monica) used an Excel spreadsheet, which was easy to update and expand, and I could refer to it quickly to compare program features. Figure 3-2 provides an example.

Figure 3-2 | **Sample Program Tracking Document**

Program name	Program A	Program B	Program C
Residency director name			
Residency director contact information			
Program size			
Teaching opportunities			
Teaching certificate			
Program setting			
College affiliation			
PGY2 programs offered			
City/address			
Salary			
Licensure requirements			
Current residents			

Conclusion

When looking for residency programs, you must first identify your interests, professional goals, and skill sets you'd like to develop. Then start searching for programs you'd like to learn more about. Online directories and residency program websites are great places to start your search.

Chapter 4

Preparing Your Curriculum Vitae

By Monica L. Miller and Deanna Kania

To effectively network and apply for residency positions, you will need a polished, well-executed curriculum vitae (CV). Your CV is a written record of your professional experiences, academics, and service activities. It may also include other information relevant to your residency search such as teaching, research experience, awards, and other accomplishments.

Like a résumé, a CV contains concise descriptions of your educational credentials and your work experience. But the CV, which is more commonly used in academic settings, is a record of all that you've done and is often several pages longer than a résumé. (For students, a CV may be four to eight pages long.) Your CV could include information about publications, research, and presentations you have given and list your memberships in professional organizations.

You will use your CV when you attend networking events such as job fairs and residency showcases and will submit it as part of residency applications. In many cases, it will serve as your introduction to the residency programs. Depending on how well your CV describes

> Your CV is a vital communication tool, so you want to craft the most up-to-date, targeted version you can.

your experiences and skills, and how accurate and clear it is, it can leave a great first impression or a less appealing one. Its quality can be a major factor in determining whether you land the interviews you desire.

Your CV is a vital communication tool, so you want to craft the most up-to-date, targeted version you can. In this chapter, you will learn strategies and tips to present your information advantageously and position yourself as someone who will be an asset to a residency program.

Purpose of Your CV

A CV tells your story, highlighting what you have done within the pharmacy profession and in other relevant areas. Residency directors and employers will use it to decide if your skills and experience make you a good fit on paper for their program. From your CV, they should be able to get a sense of what you can contribute and how successful you are likely to be in your residency position.

You can make sure your CV conveys these ideas to representatives of residency programs by including information that clearly demonstrates your skills and organizing it in a readable, logical format. In this chapter you will find important headings and sections you may want to include, pointers to make your CV represent you well, and two sample CVs.

Documenting Your Information

It is ideal to start documenting the information to include in your CV as early as possible, even during your very first year of pharmacy school. The sooner you begin to record your experiences, the less likely it is that you will forget something that might be valuable to include. If you are just beginning to pull together your CV, follow these steps:

1. Write out a list of things you have done while in pharmacy school. Think about times when you gave presentations, even during a class period, or when you helped out at an organizational event, attended a legislative event, volunteered your time, tutored a student, or participated in research.

2. After you have completed your list, have your friends, family members, and mentors review it with you. They may think of things you have done that are not included on your list.

3. Organize your activities into a CV format. You can use the examples provided in this chapter or another one that suits your personal style.

I (Monica) remember that when I was putting together my first CV, I had my dad and my mentor review it. They both recalled activities I had left out. For example, my dad reminded me about a class I had co-taught while in my last year of undergraduate school. My mentor reminded me about a presentation I'd given that I should include.

The more regularly you document your experiences, the easier it will be to keep your CV as up-to-date as possible. You can do this in a few ways.

- Keep a list or log of things that you do each month and then update your CV quarterly. Be sure to maintain this list someplace you'll remember, so you can find it when you need it.

- Maintain your list on your computer or smart phone.

- Take a few minutes after each relevant activity and quickly add it to your CV. That's what I do, because otherwise, I would forget.

No matter which method you use, update your CV frequently. Then it's always ready to go when you need it.

Creating an Effective CV

What are residency directors looking for when they review your CV? Depending on the type of residency, they may value different skills. But in general, they will be interested in learning more about your educational credentials, your clinical and work experiences, and your leadership roles. They may also want to see evidence that you can work well as a member of a team, demonstrated by participating in different group activities such as research or professional projects.

Deciding on Style and Format

Your CV can be presented in a variety of acceptable formats. To get ideas, look at many examples—from your classmates, your school's office of student services, professors, upperclassmen, professional sites online,

Sidebar 4-1. General Tips for a Well-Crafted CV

Do:
- Be concise with descriptions.

- Choose a font that is easy to read and use a 10–12 point size.

- Use the same font throughout your CV.

- Capitalize headers and put them in bold type.

- Use professional language and terminology.

- Organize information within each section in reverse chronological order.

- Use action verbs (put them in the past tense).

- Be consistent—

  - Use bulleted/fragment sentences throughout or full sentences (do not switch between the two).

  - If bullet points are used, include two to four bullets under each entry.

  - Make each entry within a section consistent, with similar information presented.

  - Use the same format for dates throughout: fully spelled out or abbreviated, with either right or left justification.

- Balance the amount of white space and type; avoid text that is too dense to read, and white space that overwhelms the page.

Don't:
- Overlook errors in spelling and grammar.

- Include—

  - Personal information (date of birth, marital status, religion).

  - Job shadowing experiences when applying for a residency or job.

  - Meeting attendance—avoid lists of the professional meetings you've attended while in pharmacy school.

  - Duplicate entries; for example, if you have presented something, include it only under "Presentations" and not in your description of the rotation during which you presented it.

Sidebar 4-1, *continued*

- Use handwriting to add missing information or corrections.

- Send out a copy of your CV electronically that still has tracked changes in it.

- Use italics to "highlight" information.

- Add colored fonts or borders.

- Use perfumed paper.

- Insert clip art or designs.

- Use unprofessional email addresses (such as notanRx@gmail.com).

---

and publications such as this one. Choose a format that appeals to you, showcases your strengths and experiences, and highlights your content in a way that is clear and readable. Your CV is unique, so only you can decide on the best format for your information.

When you look at sample CVs, you may notice helpful strategies for style and presentation. Sidebar 4-1 contains some good tips.

Organizing Your Information

Because a CV often runs four to eight pages long, you have space to cover a good amount of data. But it's important to be judicious about what you choose to include. Do not make the reader hunt for important information. Using appropriate section headers can help. You are sending a message with your CV, demonstrating to residency directors that you have the skills and experience to be successful in the positions you are targeting. To make sure your content is relevant, consider the type of residency you are applying for, whether in community pharmacy, hospital based, or managed care.

Use the list you brainstormed earlier (see the section in this chapter, "Documenting Your Information") and put a heading name next to each entry. Put the major headings you've identified within your CV and begin placing your information under the appropriate sections. Include the dates for each activity or position within your CV, and under each heading, list entries in order from most to least recent (reverse chronological order).

Once you have sketched in your relevant content under section headers, begin placing your sections in priority order. By convention, some sections have a designated spot, such as name and contact information, which always goes at the very top of your CV. Education comes next. After that, think about what you most want residency directors to notice. The sooner the information appears, the more emphasis you are giving to it.

Below is an example of an outline for a student who has major research experience, including publications and poster presentations.

- Name/Contact Information

- Education

- Professional Experience

- Advanced Pharmacy Practice Experiences (APPEs)

- Research Experience

- Publications

- Poster Presentations

- Professional Leadership/Involvement

- Presentations

- Licensure and Certifications

In this example, the student highlighted research early because it was relevant to her goals. Someone else who received a prestigious award might put the Honors and Awards section closer to the front.

The order of the headings and sections personalizes your CV and allows you to highlight what makes you unique without leaving anything out. Think about the experiences you've had that set you apart from other students and will move you higher on a residency's priority list. I (Monica) always encourage students to put licensure and certifications at the end of the CV because everyone has these.

Presenting Your Information

When you describe each of your experiences, include these details whenever possible:

- The setting.

- The population you served.

- Your supervisors' or preceptors' names and possibly members of your team.

- The clinical or health issues with which you were dealing.

- Any outcomes, achievements, or skills you gained as a result of these positions.

- The role you had within an activity or job.

Bullet Points

Presenting statements as bullet points is a great way to condense information. A list of two to four bullets immediately draws your readers' attention to the main points you want to highlight. Bullets also make your CV easier to read and give it a cleaner look than other options.

A good place to use bullet points is under your rotation and work experiences. You want to highlight key things you did using brief statements starting with strong action verbs. For example: "calculated vancomycin doses," "requested pertinent lab values that correlated to monitoring of medications," or "answered 15 drug information questions."

The following is a possible CV entry describing an APPE using bullet points. Notice that it is concise but detailed, and uses parallel construction (all verbs in the same tense, repeated grammatical structure), and action verbs.

Example:

Advanced Pharmacy Practice Experiences
    Surgical Intensive Care Unit   **August 2012**
    Indiana Hospital, Indianapolis, IN
    Jane Bertsmith, PharmD, BCPS

- Rounded daily with an interprofessional team
- Recommended medications and monitoring parameters
- Calculated total parenteral nutrition orders and vancomycin doses

If bullet points are not for you, you may also choose an alternative known as gapping, in which incomplete sentences are used to present comprehensive information concisely. For example, instead of presenting information in a narrative, you might describe a teaching assistant position this way: "Created lesson plans; graded all assignments; conducted study groups; held conferences to discuss student work."

One Section on Two Pages
Since CVs are generally four to eight pages, some of your sections might span more than one page. There are two schools of thought when this happens. Some people put the section heading only on the first page, which makes the reader assume that what follows on the next page is still within the section from the previous page. Other people repeat the section heading at the top of the new page and include the word "continued," which reminds people of the section they are reading when they flip the page.

Example:

Advanced Pharmacy Practice Experiences (Continued)

Headers/Footers
Include either headers or footers that contain your name and the page number of your CV, which allows readers to know if they have misplaced a page of your CV. Do not put a header or footer on your first page of your CV.

You can also include the last date the document was modified.

Example:

Monica L. Miller, Curriculum Vitae
Page 2 of 2   12/6/12

CV Section Headings

Organize your information under clear, descriptive headings. The following examples are commonly used, but you must tailor your headers to most effectively present your particular experiences. Looking at sample CVs is a great way to get ideas for different header titles.

Name/Contact Information

Each CV should clearly identify who you are by starting with your name as you'd like it displayed, followed by correct contact information. Your name is usually in a large bold font (use the same font that you'll use throughout the CV). Do not put "PharmD," which follows your name only after you graduate from pharmacy school, or "PharmD Candidate," which readers can infer from your education section. Information to include:

- Name (first and last with or without middle name or maiden name).

- Current and permanent address (these may be different if you move frequently).

- Email address (one that you actually check).

- Phone number (one that is actually working).

Example:

Monica L. Miller

1111 West Street
Paradise, IN 44444
Email: monicamiller@schooladdress.edu
Phone number: 555-555-5555

Education

In this section, you list undergrad, graduate, and pharmacy schools and your dates, or expected dates, of graduation. Include your degrees and any specialty training you received during your schooling. Including your grade point average (GPA) is optional; it is recommended only if you have a GPA above 3.0 on a 4-point scale. The GPA is not needed because transcripts are part of your residency application. Education is also the header under which you will put your residency training once it is under way.

Example:

Doctor of Pharmacy University of Minnesota College of Pharmacy
Graduation date: May 2012 Minneapolis, Minnesota

Bachelor of Science St. Cloud State University
Graduation date: May 2008 St. Cloud, Minnesota
   Major: Biomedical Science
   Minor: Spanish - Fluent in Conversational Spanish

Professional Experiences

This area of your CV highlights work experience you have had within the pharmacy profession and other relevant jobs, volunteer opportunities, and internships that show you have transferable skills (for example, in management, counseling, or work in global health or with specific patient populations).

Example:

Pharmacy Intern
CVS #10705 Attica, IN and #15796 Lafayette, IN Jan 2008–present
Supervisors: Mark Doe, PharmD, and Jane Dow, PharmD

Clinical Training/Advanced Pharmacy Practice Experiences

In this section, include your APPEs, introductory pharmacy practice experiences (IPPEs), and any other training you've received within pharmacy. Depending on the residency position you are applying for, you may want to consult with mentors or superiors about whether to include IPPE information. Some programs do not look at IPPEs as "experience" because they take place earlier in your pharmacy career and your responsibilities are more observational than in an APPE. One instance where it may be a good idea to include your IPPEs is if you do not have other pharmacy work experience.

Licensure and Certifications

Under this heading, list your intern's and pharmacist's licenses, including the license number(s) and date of expiration. Some programs will check your license number(s) to see if you have any violations noted by the board of pharmacy—which could be anything from medication diversion to driving under the influence of alcohol.

You could also include other relevant certifications, such as Basic Life Support, immunization delivery, Advanced Cardiac Life Support, or Pediatric Advanced Life Support. If this is your second career, include certifications you gained during your first profession such as certified public accountant or a specialty teaching certification.

Example:

California Intern Pharmacist License, #JS894SNF3, expires 11/30/2012

Optional Headings

If you have appropriate content that warrants including any of the sections below, it can enhance your CV, but do not include them if you don't have content to place under them. Having section headings that aren't filled in makes your CV look unprofessional. The reader will not know if you forgot information or if you just don't have something to include under the heading.

Publications

There are two major types of publications: peer reviewed and non-peer reviewed. Peer-reviewed publications are found in professional journals, while non-peer reviewed publications might include newsletters, professional blogs, or other media. Publishing an article or other work while in pharmacy school is a significant achievement and should be highlighted in your CV. Some programs will only count a publication that is peer-reviewed while others will also look favorably on other published materials, so include them all. You do not need to be the lead author on a publication for it to be included in your CV; any publication with your name on it is fair game. Also include any items that have been accepted for publication but have not yet gone to press.

When including a publication, list it as it would appear if referenced. Make sure to highlight your specific name if there is more than one author.

Examples:

Miller ML. MRM wrap up and a student's perspective on being a staff member. *Student Pharmacist.* 2006; January/February:8–9.

Miller ML. Are you looking for a new patient care project for your chapter? *Student Pharmacist.* In press.

Research Experience

If you have been able to participate in research, detail the projects you have worked on, those with whom you have worked, and your role.

Example:

Clindamycin vs. Vancomycin for the Treatment of Patients with Community-Acquired Methicillin-Resistant Staphylococcus Aureus (CA-MRSA) Skin and Skin Structure Infections (SSSI)   March 2007

Project: Retrospective review of 200 patients. The primary aim was to compare health outcomes among patients treated with the oral generics to those maintained on vancomycin throughout their hospital stay.

Primary Investigator: **Monica L. Miller, PharmD.** Co-Investigator: Christopher R. Frei, PharmD, MSc, BCPS

Professional Leadership/Involvement

Within this section, highlight any professional involvement and leadership positions you have had in pharmacy school organizations or college-sponsored activities, such as student council or other student organizations. In this section you can also highlight professional projects or being a reviewer for a professional journal.

Example:

American Pharmacists Association–Academy of Student Pharmacists, 2008–present
Secretary   2010–2011

Annals of Pharmacotherapy   2011–present
Reviewer

Professional Projects
Designed Diabetes, Lipid & Hypertension Brochures, Iverson Corner Drug, Bemidji, MN, July 2005

Presentations

Presentations are highly valued by residency programs, so highlight those you have given while in pharmacy school—from both the didactic portion of school and your rotations. These may include case presentations, other oral presentations such as inservices or journal clubs, or other times you formally presented information to a group of people. If you are a co-presenter of a presentation, you can either avoid listing any names or you can list your name and your co-presenters' names (last name, initials) at the end of your entry in parentheses. Include the following information:

- Presentation title.

- Location of presentation.

- Audience (you do not need exact number of attendees).

- Date.

Residency directors will be interested in learning more about your educational credentials, your clinical and work experiences, and your leadership roles.

Examples:

Diabetes and Hearing Loss. Presented in Diabetes (CLPH 490) to students and faculty at the College of Pharmacy, Purdue University, West Lafayette, IN. November 2010.

OR

Smoking Cessation
Attendees: family medicine residents
Community Family Practice Center; Indianapolis, IN.
August 2012

Poster Presentations and Abstracts

Include this section if you've had a poster presented at a professional meeting. List any poster that was presented with your name on it even if you weren't the primary presenter, whose name appears first. Poster presentation sessions typically are held at professional pharmacy organization meetings and also pharmacy schools' research days. They are used to highlight research projects that pharmacists, student pharmacists, and residents are conducting. Include the following information:

- All authors.

- Your name in bold type.

- Title of the research project.

- Full name of the meeting at which the poster was presented.

Examples:

There are different styles for these entries, as shown below.

McKanna H, Herrera C, **Miller ML**, Kimani S, Mercer T, Pastakia S, Schellhase E. De-worming Education and Treatment: A Service-Learning Experience in a Resource Constrained Setting. Urban Rise: Footprints of a Global Civilization Ecological Sciences and Engineering Symposium. West Lafayette, IN. October 2012.

OR

Proceedings from the American Association of Colleges of Pharmacy Annual Meeting, Kissimmee, FL, July 2012
Miller ML, Schellhase EM, Karwa R. Assessing Student Pharmacist Preparedness for a Global Health APPE.

Volunteer/Community Service
This section contains community service or volunteer activities in which you participate, especially those that involve populations or health issues that might be relevant to residency directors. Residency directors look for this section to see if you are interested in service within your community. They may also look in this section for you to highlight leadership roles that you've had in your service experiences—for example, if you have coached a girl's softball team, led a fundraiser, volunteered time at a women's shelter, etc. Residency directors may also look at this section to see if you have interests that are outside of pharmacy, thus making you more "well rounded." Include the following information:

- Organization name.

- Your role.

- Dates of activity.

- Location of activity.

- Bullet points or concise statements about what you did at the experience (optional).

Example:

Indiana Veteran's Home Volunteer   October 2009–2011
West Lafayette, IN

Professional Memberships

In this section, you list all the professional organizations you belong to, which is helpful not only for demonstrating your memberships, but also for helping those who read your CV to determine any memberships you have in common. (If you want to save space on your CV, you can combine this section with the section on professional leadership and involvement.) Include the following information:

- Full organization name.

- Dates you have been a member.

Example:

American Pharmacists Association   2008–present

Honors and Awards

Here's the section where you can really brag about yourself by listing honors and awards such as dean's list, semester honors, commendations for professional service, and scholarships you've received during pharmacy school. You can also include things you achieved prior to pharmacy school, especially major honors and prestigious awards. Include the following information:

- Award name.

- Date award was received.

Examples:

University of Minnesota College of Pharmacy Dean's Award   2012

Zapapas Family Merit Scholarship, Purdue University   2012

Grants and Awards

In this section, highlight grants or awards you helped to write, even if they did not get funded. On your CV, identify whether the grant was funded and if it was, how much grant money was awarded. If the grant is still under review, put a statement such as "under review" in the funding section. For grants that aren't funded, put the amount sought and say "not funded." Include the following information:

- Funding agency.

- Project/grant title.

- Your role.

- Co-investigators.

- Funding amount.

Example:

Community Service / Service Learning Grant – Purdue University Office of Engagement; September 2011
Title: Tumaini Children's Drop-In Center Jigger Treatment Project
Role: Principal Investigator
Co-investigators: Craig Vargo, Ellen Schellhase, Samuel Kimani
Funding amount: $1050

Teaching Activities

Include this section if you've had experience teaching either during or before entering pharmacy school. Teaching experiences may include being a teaching assistant for a class, giving a guest lecture, tutoring, serving as an assistant in a pharmacy school teaching lab, being a private tutor, or having a teaching career prior to attending pharmacy school. Some teaching experiences are gained through nonpharmacy experiences such as being a Sunday School teacher, volunteering to help teach English or reading in literacy programs, or giving private instrument lessons. Include the following information:

- Type of teaching and position.

- Dates of experience.

- Location.

- Number of students taught.

- Number of contact hours (hours spent face to face with the students during a given week).

- Course number (if applicable).

- Coordinator (if applicable).

Examples:

Visiting Lecturer – Cirrhosis   October 2012
Pathophysiology and Therapeutics II (CLPH 872)
Purdue University College of Pharmacy; West Lafayette, IN
Course Coordinator: Jack Dear, PharmD, BCPS
Contact hours: 2
Students: 160

Piano and Violin Teacher   June 2004–May 2010
Self-employed, West Lafayette, IN
10 piano students, 3 violin students

Other Work Experience
In this section you can include work experience that is not pharmacy related. Because some residency programs are interested in this experience, while others are focused more on your pharmacy experience, whether to include this section and what to put in it is not cut and dried. If you have worked at a place for a significant period of time—one year or more—I (Monica) suggest you list it. Also, if you had another career prior to pharmacy school, include something about it—such as your last job held—because it demonstrates your ability to balance multiple activities. Your entry should look similar to the one for pharmacy work experience. Include the following information:

- Job title.

- Employer.

- Supervisor's name.

- Dates of employment.

Example:

Food Server   December 2008–present
Olive Garden
Supervisor: Antonio Banderas

Uploading and Emailing Your CV

Because we live in an electronic era, it is important that you maintain a copy of your most up-to-date CV in a form that cannot be altered, such as a PDF, so that when you attach it to an email or upload it to a website and a reviewer opens it, you eliminate the risk of the computer system on the receiving end changing your CV's formatting. Unfortunately, if the CV formatting looks bad, it will reflect negatively on you, not on the computer system.

If you send your CV electronically as a Word (.doc or .docx) file, make sure you do not send a version that still has tracked changes left in it. Otherwise, when a reviewer opens the document, he or she will see the tracked changes right away and may get the impression that you are sloppy, do not pay attention to detail, or tend to rush through tasks.

Finalizing Your CV

After you have chosen your headers, added your information, and created concise, effective descriptions, read and polish the CV carefully. Sidebar 4-2 provides a useful checklist of things to look for. Now it's time to have trusted mentors, professional associates, faculty members, preceptors, or others review your CV and provide feedback about its readability and persuasiveness. They may be able to give you additional ideas about what to include or leave out, suggest how to phrase or format something more effectively, or recommend a choice of better headings to use.

Have them look for inconsistencies and problems with spelling and grammar. After you have worked on a document for a long time, it's very hard to pick up such errors yourself. It is important to have many eyes review your CV, including those outside the pharmacy profession. Each person will bring a different perspective to help you achieve a well-polished, professional CV you are proud to present to residency programs.

Sidebar 4-2. Checklist for Proofreading Your CV

Consider the following as you create, check, and review your CV:

☐ Are your personal details and contact information correct and current?

☐ Are all names and titles correct, with certification letters included, if applicable?

☐ Have you proofread to catch typographical or grammatical errors or spelling mistakes?

☐ Is your format uncluttered, with effective use of white space?

☐ Is your use of bold or italic type, spacing, and verb tenses consistent?

☐ Have you been consistent with your ordering (i.e., chronological versus reverse chronological)?

☐ Have you consistently spelled out or abbreviated months (i.e., October versus Oct.)?

☐ Do all of your dates align either on the right or left side?

☐ Is your language appropriately formal (no slang or abbreviations)?

☐ Have you used bullets and gapping to present information concisely?

☐ Are there any distracting stylistic elements (thick borders, multiple font styles, nonstandard bullets, etc.)?

☐ Have you included your name/page numbers in a header or footer on every page after the first?

☐ Have you had reviewers check your CV and make suggestions?

Sample CVs for a Pharmacy Residency

Two examples of CVs follow to show you differences in what each author selected to highlight, the use of bullets, and overall format of the CV. Each CV is well written and follows the general guiding principles to make a CV stand out. Do not copy these; use them as a reference.

CV Example 1

Monica L. Miller

6320 Wallard Dr., Apt C
Minneapolis, MN 46224
Phone: (444) 433-3456
Email: miller5@placeuniversity.edu

PROFESSIONAL EDUCATION / TRAINING

Doctor of Pharmacy　　　　　University of Minnesota College of Pharmacy
Graduation date: May 2006　　　Minneapolis, MN

Bachelor of Science　　　　　St. Cloud State University
Graduation date: May 2002　　　St. Cloud, MN
　Major: Biomedical Science
　Minor: Chemistry

PHARMACY PRACTICE EXPERIENCE

Pharmacy Intern　　　　　　　　　　　**May 2004–May 2006**
Regions Hospital, St. Paul, MN
Supervisor: Peggy Raven, PharmD
Responsibilities: Prepared IVs, chemotherapy & TPNs, stocked Pyxis &
satellite pharmacies, fielded & answered questions posed by nurses

Pharmacy Technician　　　　　　　　　**May 1999–August 2002**
Pharmerica Pharmacy, Sioux Falls, SD
Supervisor: Kari Konders-Shandards, RPh
Responsibilities: Handled order entry & clarification, filled prescriptions
& cyclic fills, compounded

ADVANCED PHARMACY PRACTICE EXPERIENCES

Acute Care　　　　　　　　　　　　　**February–April 2006**
Children's Hospitals, St. Paul, MN
Preceptor: Laura Garry, PharmD, BCPS

Inpatient Psychiatric Patient Care　　　**January 2006**
University Medical Center
Preceptor: Robert German, PharmD

Cardiovascular Ambulatory Care Clinic　　**November 2005**
VA Medical Center, West Palm Beach, FL
Preceptor: David Ranger, PharmD, BCPS

CV Example 1, *continued*

Community Practice & Patient Care   May–July 2005
Iverson Corner Drug, Bemidji, MN
Preceptor: Paul George, RPh

Home Care/Infusion Pharmacy   May–July 2005
Progressive Health Care, Bemidji, MN
Preceptor: Paul George, RPh

Association Management   October 2005
American Pharmacists Association, Washington, DC
Preceptor: Oscar Allan, PharmD

Ambulatory Care & Institutional Practice   August–September 2005
Paynesville Area Health Care System, Paynesville, MN
Preceptor: Tammy Orange, PharmD

TEACHING ACTIVITIES

Teaching Assistant, Pharmaceutical Care Learning Center
                                                         May 2004–May 2005
PHR: 6173 105 second-year student pharmacists, fall term
PHR: 6174 105 second-year student pharmacists, spring term
University of Minnesota College of Pharmacy
Student contact & grading time: 8 hours per week
Course Coordinator: Troy Graham, PharmD

Chemistry 101 Joint Teacher   January–May 2002
Chemistry 101: 10 students
St. Cloud State University, Chemistry Department
Student contact & grading time: 2 hours per week

PLATFORM / INVITED SPEAKER PRESENTATIONS

NATIONAL

Common Sense, Interprofessional Teams
Attendees: Student pharmacists, medical students, nursing students, &
staff members
Paul Ambrose Health Promotion Student Leadership Symposium,
Washington, DC; June 26, 2005

continued on page 70

CV Example 1, *continued*

PLATFORM / INVITED SPEAKER PRESENTATIONS, *continued*

National Case Competition Invitation
Attendees: Medical school deans from various academic health centers
Institute for Health Care Improvement Meeting, Memphis, TN;
October 27–28, 2004

4th Year Member Recruitment
Attendees: Student pharmacists
APhA Annual Meeting, Seattle, WA; April 2004

REGIONAL

Panel Member, Quality Improvement Panel Discussion on Team Collaboration
Attendees: Physicians, pharmacists, students, & management
Mayo Medical School, Rochester, MN; September 14, 2005

LOCAL

CLARION
Attendees: Medical school deans from various academic health centers
Institute for Health Care Improvement Medical School Collaborative,
Minneapolis, MN; May 5, 2004

Student Perspectives on Pharmacy
Attendees: Pre-pharmacy students
The University of Minnesota, Pharmacy 1001, Minneapolis, MN; September 2003

The Ideal Pharmaceutical Care Curriculum
Attendees: Pharmacy faculty & student pharmacists
Deep Portage Pharmaceutical Care Conference 2nd Annual, Hackensack, MN;
February 2003

PRESENTATIONS

Pulmonary Embolism
Attendees: Pharmacists & pharmacy practice residents
Weekly pharmacists' meeting, University Hospital, San Antonio, TX;
October 18, 2006

Acute Coronary Syndrome and Ischemic Heart Disease
Attendees: Pharmacy practice residents, pharmacists, & student pharmacists
Advanced Pharmacotherapy, UTHSCSA, San Antonio, TX; September 29, 2006

CV Example 1, *continued*

PRESENTATIONS, *continued*

Hematopoetic Stem Cell Transplant and Neutropenic Fever Case Presentation
Attendees: Pharmacists & residents
Weekly pharmacists' meeting, United Hospital, Minneapolis, MN; May 4, 2006

Interprofessional Teams and a Pharmacist's Role on Them
Attendees: Pharmacists & student pharmacists
PharmD Four Seminar Class, University of Minnesota, Minneapolis, MN;
April 24, 2006

Myasthenia Gravis
Attendees: Pharmacists & residents
Weekly pharmacists' meeting, United Hospital, Minneapolis, MN; March 5, 2006

Weight Gain and Atypical Antipsychotics
Attendees: Pharmacists & student pharmacists
Journal club meeting, Riverside Hospital, Minneapolis, MN; February 20, 2006

Pharmacotherapy Review of Heart Transplant Medications
Attendees: Pharmacists & student pharmacists
Staff meeting, West Palm Beach, VA; West Palm Beach, FL; December 20, 2005

RESEARCH

Interprofessional Teams: Definition, Characteristics, Pharmacist's Roles, & Barriers Encountered   January 2006
Project: Performed a literature review on interprofessional teams. The main research questions were: (i) what is a patient centered "interprofessional team"; and (ii) what are the pharmacist's roles on interprofessional/collaborative health care teams. The literature also reveals important issues to consider such as common characteristics and barriers encountered in the formation of an interprofessional team.
    Primary Investigator: Monica L. Miller
    Advisors: Barbara F. Brandt, PhD & Todd Sorensen, PharmD

International Pharmaceutical Care Curriculum Research   May–August 2003
Project: Traveling throughout the United Kingdom interviewing pharmacists in various pharmacy settings about pharmaceutical care and their attitudes toward an international pharmacy curriculum.
    Co-Investigators: Monica L. Miller & Victoria Losinski
    Advisor: Linda M. Strand, PharmD

continued on page 72

CV Example 1, *continued*

GRANTS AND AWARDS

Samuel W. Melendy Research Scholarship: $5000　　　**May 2003**
International Pharmaceutical Care
Role: Co-investigator (Victoria Losinski)
Research grant used to fund international pharmaceutical care curriculum in summer of 2003

PUBLICATIONS

Miller ML. MRM wrap up and a student's perspective on being a staff member. *Student Pharmacist.* 2006; January/February:8–9.

Miller ML. Are you looking for a new patient care project for your chapter? *Pharmacy Student.* 2004; November/December:36–37.

PROFESSIONAL LEADERSHIP & MEMBERSHIPS

American College of Clinical Pharmacy (ACCP)	**2006–present**
Association of Clinicians for the Underserved (ACU)	**2005–2006**
1st Student Pharmacist Board Member	2005–2006
Institute of Health Care Improvement (IHI)	**2004–present**
Student Initiated Learning Quality Improvement Committee	2004–2005
Clinician Administrator Relationship Organization (CLARION)	**2003–2006**
Education Chair	2004–2005
National Case Competition Planner	2004–2005
Secretary	2003–2004
Participant: Case Competition	2003
Phi Lambda Sigma (PLS)	**2003–present**
Leadership Proposal Writer, Professionalism Toolkit	2004
American Society of Health-System Pharmacists (ASHP)	**2002–present**
Minnesota Pharmacists Association (MPhA)	**2002–present**
MPhA Awards Committee Member	2005–2006
Bulldog Grassroots Legislative Group Member	2004–2006
MPhA Board of Directors Member	2004–2005

CV Example 1, *continued*

PROFESSIONAL LEADERSHIP & MEMBERSHIPS, *continued*

American Pharmacists Association Academy of Student Pharmacists (APhA-ASP)   2002–present

National Education Standing Committee Vice Chair	2005–2006
Slated National Member-at-large Candidate	April 2005
Attendee, Utah School on Alcoholism and Substance Abuse	June 2004
National President Elect Candidate	March 2004
Region V Member-at-large	2003–2004

Minnesota Pharmacy Student Alliance (MPSA)   2002–2006
(Jointly Represents APhA, ASHP, MPhA, MSHP, NCPA)

President	2004–2005
Membership Vice President	2003–2004
IPSF Liaison	2003–2004
Participant:	2002–2005

Operation Diabetes, Operation Immunization, Katy's Kids, OTC Case Competition & Stroke Prevention

University of Minnesota College of Pharmacy   2002–2006

Tour guide for pharmacy preview day & interview days	2002–2005
Panel member, interview days	2002–2005
Usher, awards banquet, 1st year white coat ceremony	2003, 2004
Marshal for 3rd year white coat ceremony	2003
Pre-professional Student Mentor	2004–2005
Student Representative, Faculty Search Committee	2004
Student Representative, Technology Committee	2002–2003
Member, Student Group for ACPE Accreditation Visit	2003

Professional Projects

Designed Diabetes, Lipid & Hypertension Brochures, Iverson Corner Drug, Bemidji, MN, July 2005

Created a working hospital formulary document, Paynesville Area Health Care System, Paynesville, MN, August 2005

Cost benefit analysis of warfarin versus enoxaparin use in knee replacement patients, Paynesville, MN, September 2005

COMMUNITY SERVICE

Coached, Under 10 Girls Soccer	2005

continued on page 74

CV Example 1, *continued*

HONORS & AWARDS

Travel Scholarship, University of Texas College of Pharmacy	2007
University of Minnesota College of Pharmacy Dean's Award	2006
APhA-ASP Senior Recognition Award	2006
APhA Student Leadership Award	2005
MPhA/MPSA President's Award	2005
Minnesota Pharmacist's Foundation Outstanding Student Scholarship	2004, 2005
Who's Who of College Students	2003, 2004, 2005

LICENSURE & CERTIFICATIONS

Pharmacy intern, Minnesota Board of Pharmacy, License # HJ34ST645 (active)	2003–2006
BLS CPR Certified	2004–present
Adult Immunization Certified Delivery-Certified Provider	2004–present

CV Example 2

Sam R. Thomas

SRThomas@hotmail.com
555-555-5555
4765 Eagle Creek Pkwy
Temple, IN 45555

EDUCATION

Doctor of Pharmacy   Purdue University
Graduation: May 2011   West Lafayette, IN

LICENSURE and CERTIFICATION

Pharmacy Intern, Indiana, #ST45389021 American Society for Clinical Pathology
Certified, CT (ASCP), Certification #55467

PROFESSIONAL PHARMACY EXPERIENCE

Internships

Apr 2010–Jun 2011   **Pharmacy Intern**
                           Witham Hospital, Lebanon, IN
                           Supervisor: Joe Bitner, RPh
                           • Monitored patients receiving anticoagulation
                             therapy
                           • Assisted with vancomycin dosing and monitoring
                           • Clarified and entered orders

May–Aug 2009   **Pharmacy Intern**
                           St. Joseph Hospital, Kokomo, IN
                           Supervisor: Jim Silver, RPh
                           • Pulled medications and stocked Pyxis®
                           • Assisted with preparation of IVs and TPNs
                           • Prepared and updated various pharmacy forms

May–Aug 2008   **Pharmacy Intern**
                           Cardinal Health Nuclear Pharmacy, Indianapolis, IN
                           Supervisor: Keith Koontz, RPh
                           • Drew up, wiped, and surveyed unit doses
                           • Performed quality control testing
                           • Assisted with stocking delivery cases

continued on page 76

CV Example 2, *continued*

WORK EXPERIENCE

Mar 2004–Aug 2007   **Cytotechnologist**
Department of Pathology and Laboratory Medicine
RL Roudebush VA Medical Center, Indianapolis, IN
Supervisor: Andrea VonIns, CT (ASCP)
- Accessioned, prepared, and screened non-GYN and GYN specimens
- Assisted with fine needle aspiration biopsy procedures

Aug 2003–Mar 2004   **Research Cytotechnologist**
Department of Pathology and Laboratory Medicine
Indiana University School of Medicine, Indianapolis, IN
Supervisor: Liang Cheng, MD
- Performed laser capture and manual tissue microdissection
- Ran polymerase chain reaction on harvested tissue
- Assisted with agarose and polyacrylamide gel electrophoresis

ADVANCED PHARMACY PRACTICE EXPERIENCES
Pending

Nov 2010   **Emergency Medicine**
Carolinas Medical Center, North Concord, NC
Preceptor: Andrea Jones, PharmD

Dec 2010–Jan 2011   **Community Operations**
Payless Pharmacy #843, Lafayette, IN
Preceptor: Pamela Josh, RPh

Mar 2011   **Critical Care**
Memorial Hospital, Indianapolis, IN
Preceptor: Michael Joseph, PharmD, BCPS

Apr 2011   **Ambulatory Care**
Memorial Hospital, Indianapolis, IN
Preceptor: Tim Thumb, PharmD, BCPS, CDE

CV Example 2, *continued*

ADVANCED PHARMACY PRACTICE EXPERIENCES, *continued*

Completed

Oct 2010

Drug Information
Memorial Hospital, Indianapolis, IN
Preceptor: Adam Jackson, PharmD
- Responded to drug information requests
- Authored a drug monograph for formulary addition

Sept 2010

Adult Medicine
Memorial Hospital, Indianapolis, IN
Preceptor: Jeremy Chris, PharmD, BCPS (AQ Cardiology), FCCP, FAPhA
- Participated in daily patient-care rounds with interprofessional medical team
- Monitored patients vancomycin levels

Aug 2010

Ambulatory Care
Community Health Center, Lafayette, IN
Preceptor: Carole Johnson, PharmD
- Adjusted medication regimens in both the adult and pediatric setting
- Counseled patients on various medications

July 2010

Hospital Operations
Arnett Hospital, Lafayette, IN
Preceptor: Aaron Miller, PharmD
- Participated daily in multidisciplinary ICU rounds
- Documented 10 interventions weekly

June 2010

Long-Term Care/Geriatrics
Mr. Drugs, Crawfordsville, IN
Preceptor: Patrick Joseph, RPh
- Performed medication regimen reviews; recommended changes to therapy
- Participated in monthly behavior meeting Prepared and checked medication orders

continued on page 78

CV Example 2, *continued*

May 2010   **Administrative/Academic**
                        The University College of Pharmacy
                        Preceptor: Steven Crowe, PharmD, FASHP
                        - Created interactive exercise for and administered
                          the DiSC Profile to Dean of Students faculty
                          retreat
                        - Assisted with financial projections for the
                          Department of Pharmacy Practice

PUBLICATIONS

Thomas S: Coumadin Dosing, Monitoring and Management. *Pharmacy Newsletter.* St. Joseph Hospital, Kokomo, IN, August 2009

Thomas S: Heparin-Induced Thrombocytopenia (HIT): A Brief Overview. *Pharmacy Newsletter.* St. Joseph Hospital, Kokomo, IN, January 2009

POSTER PRESENTATIONS

Carr MD, Zhang S, Eble JN, Lopez-Beltran A, **Thomas S**, Cheng L. Clonal origin of multiple lymph node metastases in patients with solitary bladder carcinomas. United States and Canadian Academy of Pathology Annual Meeting, Mar 2004

McCarthy RP, Zhang S, Eble JN, Lopez-Beltran A, Yang XJ, MacLennan GT, Nigro K, Pan C, **Thomas S**, Cheng L. Concordant genetic alterations in the urinary bladder small cell carcinomas and co-existing urothelial carcinoma. United States and Canadian Academy of Pathology Annual Meeting, Mar 2004

Thomas S, Barrett K, Coy T, Crabtree W. The efficacy of urine cytology for the detection of urothelial carcinoma in a large academic hospital. American Society of Cytopathology Annual Meeting, Nov 2002

PRESENTATIONS

Apr 2011   **ADHD Medications**
             Attendees: pharmacists, medical residents, attending pediatrician
             Methodist Hospital, Indianapolis, IN

Mar 2011   **Insulin: A Brief Overview**
             Attendees: patients, pharmacists, rotation students
             Riverview Hospital, Noblesville, IN

CV Example 2, *continued*

PRESENTATIONS, *continued*

Nov 2010	***Clostridium difficile* 2010 Clinical Practice Guidelines Update** Attendees: pharmacists, rotation students Hendricks Regional Health, Danville, IN
Nov 2010	**Patient Case: Fungal Pneumonia** Attendees: pharmacists, rotation students Hendricks Regional Health, Danville, IN
Sept 2010	**Uloric® (febuxostat)** Attendees: pharmacists, resident, rotation students Wishard Hospital, Indianapolis, IN
Jun 2010	**Newly Diagnosed HIV/AIDS** Attendees: pharmacists, residents, rotation students Wishard Hospital, Indianapolis, IN
May 2010	**Patient Case: CHF Exacerbation** Attendees: Purdue College of Pharmacy Associate Dean for Clinical Programs, faculty and staff, rotation students Wishard Hospital, Indianapolis, IN
Jun 2009	**A Brief Insulin Review** Attendees: Trinity House Behavioral Services nursing staff St. Joseph Hospital Pharmacy, Kokomo, IN
Jan 2009	**Heparin-Induced Thrombocytopenia (HIT): An Overview** Attendees: pharmacists St. Joseph Hospital Pharmacy, Kokomo, IN
Nov 2003	**Diagnostic Cytology Seminar Cases** Attendees: pathologists and cytotechnologists Cytology Society of Indiana Fall Meeting, Indianapolis, IN

PROFESSIONAL INVOLVEMENT

Jun 2006–Aug 2007	**Indianapolis VA Anatomic Pathology Chemical Inventory** • Project Leader • Created instructional packets for teams of employees • Monitored and communicated progress to supervisor

continued on page 80

CV Example 2, *continued*

PROFESSIONAL INVOLVEMENT, *continued*

Jun 2006–Jul 2006   **Backpack Attack Back-to-School Supply Drive, Indianapolis, IN**
- Project Leader
- Led Indianapolis VA laboratory-wide school supply drive
- Coordinated donations with other area organizations

PROFESSIONAL ORGANIZATIONS

2008–2011   **American Society of Consultant Pharmacists**
2009–2010   Treasurer

2008–2011   **Indiana Pharmacists Alliance**

2009–2010   **Purdue Student Society of Health-System Pharmacists**
2009   Co-Chair, Diabetes Outreach

2007–2008   **Society of Nuclear Pharmacy**

HONORS

2010–2011   **Raymond A. McCullough Pharmacy Scholarship,** Purdue University

Fall 2007–Spring 2011   **Dean's List**, Purdue University

Jan 2007   **Special Contribution Award,** Richard L. Roudebush VA Medical Center

Dec 2006   **Superior Performance Award,** Richard L. Roudebush VA Medical Center

Fall 2002, Spring 2003   **Dean's List**, Indiana University

VOLUNTEER EXPERIENCE

Nov 2009   **Indiana Veterans' Home Senior Health Fair**
West Lafayette, IN
- Assisted with setup and teardown of event
- Discussed diabetes and nutrition with residents

CV Example 2, *continued*

VOLUNTEER EXPERIENCE, *continued*

Jan–Feb 2008   **Indiana Ombudsman Program**
West Lafayette, IN
- Visited with long-term-care facility residents
- Reported resident and facility conditions to volunteer coordinator

Jun 2006–Mar 2007   **Indiana Reading and Information Services**
Indianapolis, IN
- Read books for broadcast to blind and print-impaired in central Indiana

Oct 2006   **American Cancer Society Making Strides Against Breast Cancer Walk**
Indianapolis, IN
- Performed general setup duties

Sept–Dec 2005   **College Park Disabled Ministry**
Indianapolis, IN
- Helped with transport of disabled to and from church
- Assisted with food, drink, note taking, mobility, medication, and communion

Chapter 5

Connecting with Residency Programs

By Molly A. Mason, Monica L. Miller, and Deanna Kania

After you've researched the programs you're interested in and have narrowed your list, it is time to connect with the residency programs. One of the best ways to learn more about residency programs is to talk with the people who organize and participate in them, which is possible in a few ways:

- Attending residency showcases.

- Attending national and state meetings.

- Communicating with program representatives.

This chapter gives advice about making contact with residency programs, including events to attend, questions to ask, and ways to make your interaction successful.

What Is a Residency Showcase?

A residency showcase is a professional event where program directors, residents, and other residency representatives are available to answer questions about their program. These events are typically held during regional, state, and national pharmacy meetings, but individual colleges of pharmacy sometimes

Candidates can stand out during a residency showcase if they know about my program ahead of time and do enough research to ask good questions. It helps if they've contacted me or my past residents beforehand, even if they just shoot us a quick email. I like for students to come prepared with questions not only for me, but for my current resident, as well—especially some professional questions and some "personality" questions. So much of what makes a residency successful is when the resident's personality meshes with the preceptor's.

*—Patty Elsner,
Residency Director,
Walgreens*

hold them in conjunction with a career fair or as stand-alone events. Each showcase varies in size depending on the number of programs participating and the volume of attendees. Typically a showcase lasts about two hours.

At these events, usually held in a large ballroom or meeting room, residency programs are given booth space about the size of a large table to display posters or banners with their program name and some program details. Each booth is usually staffed with program representatives such as the residency director, current residents, and preceptors. See Sidebar 5-1 for general tips on interacting with programs.

> To navigate residency showcases, plan which program representatives you want to speak with first.

Your role as an attendee and potential candidate is to approach the booth and talk with program representatives. It's a great opportunity to ask questions and get more details about their residency program. (Sidebar 5-2 provides sample questions.) You will likely be given brochures or even flash drives with information you can take home and review at your leisure. Before attending a residency showcase event, try to get from the host school or organization a list of the programs that will be represented.

Attendance at residency showcases can sometimes be free for residency candidates, but more commonly there is a fee, which tends to be lower if you register in advance. However, you can usually sign up for these events on site the day they are held, as well. To learn the cost, verify details with the event's host organization or check the emails or notices advertising the event.

Residency showcases can be packed and loud, filled with other students, with everyone talking at once. To navigate these events, plan which program representatives you want to speak with first, because you might not have time to talk with everyone. In addition, you may have to wait to speak with members of a residency program if they are busy talking with other interested candidates. Be patient and polite while waiting.

Residency showcases at annual meetings of state pharmacy associations and those offered by colleges of pharmacy usually feature programs from within the state and surrounding areas. Most state association meetings

---

Sidebar 5-1. Tips for Interacting with Program Representatives at a Residency Showcase

- Be professional during the whole meeting.

- Each event is only a few hours long, so manage your time well.

- Ask pointed questions of the residency directors and residents (see Sidebar 5-2).

- Keep interactions brief; spend enough time to get answers to important questions, but allow time to talk with other program representatives.

- Don't monopolize a program representative; other students will want time to talk with the representatives for the program in which you are interested.

- Focus on your own plan and do not let competitive behavior from other students stress you out.

---

also host small group sessions for students to discuss topics such as networking, presentation and interview skills, and pharmacist licensure exams. Regional residency showcases, limited to a few states, typically host approximately 20 to 30 programs.

The following national associations offer residency showcases in conjunction with annual meetings. See Table 5-1 for more details.

- **American College of Clinical Pharmacy (ACCP)** holds its Residency and Fellowship during the ACCP's annual meeting, held in October. Go to www.accp.com

- **Academy of Managed Care Pharmacy (AMCP)** hosts its Managed Care Residency Showcase during its yearly Education Conference in October. Go to www.amcp.org

- **American Pharmacists Association (APhA)** offers residency showcases in conjunction with the Academy of Student Pharmacists Midyear Regional Meetings (MRMs), held each fall in eight regions across the country. APhA also offers a national showcase in the spring during the Annual Meeting and Exposition. Go to www.pharmacist.com

- **American Society of Health-System Pharmacists (ASHP)**
  presents the largest Residency Showcase of them all, held in
  early December in conjunction with its Midyear Clinical Meeting
  (MCM). Go to www.ashp.org. More details on the ASHP Residency
  Showcase appear later in this chapter.

- **National Community Pharmacists Association (NCPA)** offers
  the Community Pharmacy Residency Showcase at its Annual
  Convention and Trade Exhibition, typically held in October.
  Go to www.ncpanet.org

Sidebar 5-2. What to Ask about Residency Programs

Before you connect with residency program representatives—whether in person,
by telephone, or by email—prepare a list of questions to ask. To devise effective
questions, base them on the professional goals you have identified, as recommended in Chapter 3, and get input from your mentors. Armed with these questions,
you can assess which programs are most likely to help you meet your goals.

Below are sample questions. It's a long list, and you will not have time to ask
each program representative every question. Prioritize your questions and ask
the ones that pertain directly to your career goals first. If you're at a residency
showcase and you run out of time, you can send follow-up questions to
residency representatives by email. These questions can also be asked during
an onsite interview.

Questions for All Program Representatives
- How many residents have graduated from your program?

- What are past residents doing now?

- Are residents assigned a mentor?

- Are program residents required to participate in an on-call program?

- Does the technology in your setting offer easy access to patient data?

- How is the residency project chosen?

- What types of residency projects have residents done in the past?

- What are the expectations of the residency project? Does it result in
  publication, a poster presentation, or some other product?

Sidebar 5-2, *continued*

- What is the nature of patient care provided? For example, does the resident participate in rounding services?

- What type of collaboration do pharmacists have with other health care professionals?

- What are the elective opportunities?

- How are electives selected?

- Is there an option for an international elective?

- Is career planning addressed during the program?

- What types of teaching experiences are offered?

- Is participation in a teaching certificate program offered?

- What plans does the pharmacy program have to expand its role at the institution where it is housed?

- What attracted you (the preceptors) to this practice site?

- Do the residents head or sit on any committees?

- What level of progression have you seen in your residents as they move through the program?

- What do you do to ensure that preceptors continue to develop precepting skills?

- Are residents reimbursed for meeting attendance?

- Is participation in state or national organizations encouraged?

- Is membership in professional organizations paid for?

- What percentage of beds are filled on average (hospital daily census)?

- What does it take for a resident to be successful in this program?

- How are you able to modify the rotation schedule to each resident's skills and career goals?

- Will I be encouraged to obtain further certifications?

- Will I learn to set up a pharmacy practice site (the ins and outs of billing and other operational concerns)?

continued on page 88

Sidebar 5-2. What to Ask about Residency Programs,
continued

Questions for Residency Directors
- What are your goals for the residency program?

- What are some strengths of the program?

- What are some weaknesses of the program and how have you planned to address them?

- How do you help residents develop strong skills and overcome their weaknesses?

- What is your relationship like with the residents?

Questions for Residents
- If you were to choose all over again, would you still select this program?

- Please describe a typical week.

- In what ways have you grown as a pharmacist during your experience so far?

- What do you really like about this program?

- What would you like to see improved?

- How often do you have meetings with the residency director to assess your progress through the program?

- What areas of professional growth have you experienced?

- What would you have liked to know before starting the program that you didn't know?

- Has your program director created an environment where you feel you can be honest about your thoughts and feelings?

- Has the program adapted and been flexible as your interests have changed?

- Please describe the extent of mentoring you have received. Are you happy with this?

- How prepared do you feel for your next career step?

Table 5-1 | National Residency Showcases

Meeting Characteristics	ACCP	AMCP	APhA		ASHP	NCPA
			MRM	Annual Meeting		
Attendees	Clinical pharmacists Faculty Residents Students Fellows	Managed care pharmacists Students Residents Faculty	Students Some faculty	Students Pharmacists Residents Fellows Faculty	Residents Students Fellows Faculty Residency Directors Health-system pharmacists	Community pharmacists Students Residents
Month	October	October	October/November	March/April	Early December	October
Showcase Exhibitors	Residencies Fellowships Graduate Programs	Managed care residencies Fellowships	Residencies Fellowships	Residencies (mostly community pharmacy)	Residencies (PGY1 and PGY2)	Community pharmacy residencies
Showcase Cost	Free with meeting registration	Free with meeting registration	Free with meeting registration	Free with meeting registration	Free with meeting registration	Free with meeting registration
Showcase Length	1 showcase time; ~2 hours	1 showcase time; ~2 hours	1 showcase time; ~2 hours	1 showcase time; ~2 hours	3 showcase times; 3.5 hours each	1 showcase time; ~2 hours
Unique Features	- Exhibitor list online - Programs can contact students before the meeting - Able to communicate with fellowship and graduate school programs - Some open job postings	- Focus on managed care residencies and fellowships - Smaller showcase	- Regional exhibitors - Less expensive than national meetings - Primarily student attendees	- Showcase occurs in March/April after the match submissions are due - Exhibits many community pharmacy residency programs	- Largest residency showcase - Residencies exhibiting from all over the U.S. - Crowded	- Smaller, more intimate meeting - Exhibits only community pharmacy residency programs

ASHP Residency Showcase

This showcase is huge. It's a wonderful resource, but it's also crowded and can feel chaotic if you do not prepare in advance. In 2011, for example, the ASHP Residency Showcase had representatives recruiting for more than 1100 pharmacy residency programs.[1] And the MCM, where the Residency Showcase takes place, is huge, too, with nearly 20,000 pharmacists from the United States and the entire world attending each year.[1]

Because the ASHP Residency Showcase is so large, it is divided into three different sessions that last three hours each. Each program is displayed in only one of the three sessions, which are held Monday afternoon, Tuesday morning, and Tuesday afternoon. With approximately 200 programs per session, it's inevitable that programs you are interested in will be displaying at the same time. It's important to do your research and know which programs will be displayed during which time period, so you can visit those that interest you the most. Your interaction with each program will be brief (maybe 10 minutes or less), which should allow you to talk with multiple programs during the three hours.

Many students wonder if it makes sense to attend the ASHP Residency Showcase if they know they plan to limit their choices to one geographic area. The best way to answer that question is to contact programs within your area in advance and ask if they will be participating in residency showcases closer to you, such as at state meetings or at career fairs at nearby schools.

For tips on how to prepare and get the most out of the ASHP Residency Showcase, see Sidebar 5-3.

Navigating Professional Meetings

Residency showcases are not isolated events; typically they are held in conjunction with professional pharmacy meetings as part of the programming being offered. You pay one registration fee to attend the whole thing—meeting and showcase. You will interact with many different people at these meetings, including practicing pharmacists and pharmacy leaders, who will be in the residency showcase, as well.

Sidebar 5-3. Getting the Most from the ASHP Residency Showcase

Weeks or Days Beforehand

- Do enough research to identify programs that interest you the most. (See Chapter 3 for more details.)

- Learn the names of residency directors at your programs of interest.

- Prepare a "cheat sheet" of notes about each of your preferred programs to take to the showcase.

- Prepare a list of open-ended questions (see Sidebar 5-2).

- Obtain business cards to exchange with people you meet.

- Prepare and print copies of your CV to take.

- Plan a professional outfit to wear.

- Review the residency directory. See Chapter 3 for a listing of national associations with online directories of residency programs.

- Know when the programs that most interest you will be displayed. (See the ASHP website for the schedule.)

- Plan a strategy for each of the three Residency Showcase time slots.

- Print a floor plan for each session to help navigate the room (it is posted on the ASHP website prior to the meeting).

At the Showcase

- You will be on your feet for long stretches, so wear comfortable walking shoes.

- Carry a professional work bag to hold your CV and personal items—and to store the literature you pick up.

- Bring a bottle of water and snacks in your bag, because these items are expensive at convention centers.

- Bring other small items to ensure your comfort and "presentability," such as lip balm, tissues, and breath mints.

- Don't stand by passively waiting for program representatives to talk with you. Walk up to the program representative, introduce yourself (without interrupting a conversation in progress), and ask a question.

continued on page 92

Sidebar 5-3. Getting the Most from the ASHP Residency Showcase, *continued*

- Using the list in Sidebar 5-2 as a guide, ask a few questions when you stop by the program booths. Ask the same questions at each program, so you can compare "apples with apples." Talk with both preceptors and residents to get varied perspectives. Be sure to ask residents what they like about the program.

- Leave a résumé and business card with the program director or other program representative if the director is not present.

- Bring a notepad or paper and pens to jot answers to questions, observations about programs, and other important notes.

After the Showcase
- Write notes about each program after you talk with the representative (not as he or she is talking) and start digesting the information in preparation for deciding where you will submit applications.

- Send thank-you letters to program representatives you interacted with at the showcase.

- Begin working on your application, including your letter of intent (see Chapter 6).

When attending professional meetings, always be professional. You don't always know the person with whom you are interacting, especially at social functions—and you don't want them to remember you for the wrong reasons. Pharmacy is a small world, and many pharmacists have professional networks that stretch across the country. These pharmacists talk with friends and peers about interactions they've had with students at work, on rotation, or during professional events. It's natural to want to share firsthand knowledge about those who are "up and coming" in the profession. Keep in mind that pharmacists you meet may later speak highly or negatively of you, depending on your behavior. It's your responsibility to make sure they have only good things to say. (I've actually heard of students not being granted a residency interview because they were seen partying too much and getting out of control at the ASHP MCM.)

> When attending professional meetings, always be professional. You don't always know the person with whom you are interacting.

People will observe your actions from the minute the meeting starts to the time you get back to your own city. You will likely make an impression even on those you don't meet or engage in conversation. Professional meetings can be a lot of fun, with a mix of social and learning activities. Enjoy yourself, but focus on your career goals and never forget that leaders and decision makers will remember how you conduct yourself. Your worst case scenario would be if someone who interviewed you for a coveted residency slot were to see you do something you are not proud of—and consequently decide not to hire you.

- If you drink alcohol, keep it to a minimum. Do not become inebriated while at the meeting, and do not attend the residency showcase or interviews with alcohol on your breath or without showering from the night before.

- Do not badmouth people or programs. If you feel a need to express opinions to your friends or fellow attendees, do so only in private—in your hotel room with the door securely closed.

- Do not grab excessive quantities of free giveaways during the exhibition. Talk politely and professionally to the exhibitors about their products.

- Be sure that your social networking sites, such as Facebook and Twitter, are professional before you attend a professional meeting, because people you meet are likely to look you up. Consider taking your page down or changing the settings so everything is private. Your profile picture should not show you holding an alcoholic beverage, posed provocatively, or doing anything that casts you in a negative light.

- Attend student programming sessions to network with your colleagues across the country and learn more about the profession.

- Network with everyone you meet during a meeting; collect contact information, preferably by swapping business cards.

- Attend poster sessions, which allow you to learn about the latest research being conducted by students, residents, and pharmacists. When viewing a poster, make sure to ask at least one question. The person standing by the poster will appreciate that someone took time to inquire about his or her research.

Sidebar 5-4. Tips for Connecting with Residencies by Email

A great way to communicate with residency programs—whether to make initial contact, get key information, or ask follow-up questions—is through email. It's easy and direct, and using email gives you a written record of the information you receive. Below are a few tips, followed by a sample email.

1. Be professional in your email communications. Your messages will likely be saved and referred to during the interview process.

2. Do not ask questions whose answers can be found easily on the program's website.

3. In your email, express your interest in the program.

4. Keep your subject line professional and informative, such as "Inquiry about your PGY1 residency program."

Sample Email to a Resident from Your School

Subject: Fellow Purdue Student Seeking Residency Information

Dear Dr. _____,

My name is _____ and I am a P4 at Purdue University. We were both members of APhA-ASP and attended some of the same meetings. I thought it would be helpful to contact a familiar face about University Medical Center's residency program, which interests me greatly.

I know you are busy, but can you spare a few minutes to answer some questions for me by email? I'd love to hear your insights into the dynamics of the program.

• What can you tell me about your experience so far? What are the plusses and minuses?

• I have an interest in academia and ambulatory care. Can you share information on the quality/quantity of the educational and ambulatory care components of the residency?

• What are your thoughts on the mentorship you've experienced so far?

I hope you are having a great year, and thank you for your help!

Sincerely,

Your Name

- Attend receptions sponsored by pharmacy schools and colleges to network and show your interest. If a representative from a particular residency program invites you to a reception, *go to it*. While there, ask to speak with past residents and people in the program you haven't previously met.

ASHP Personnel Placement Service

Students often ask, what is the Personnel Placement Service (PPS)? Do I need to participate in it if I am applying for a PGY1 residency?

In answer to the first question, PPS is a recruitment program that takes place during the ASHP MCM. Residency recruiters (usually the residency program directors), job recruiters, and representatives from industry fellowships use the PPS to meet with prospective candidates in 30-minute one-on-one introductory sessions. These brief meetings allow both parties to get a feel for each other and decide if an on-site interview is warranted.

Prior to the meeting, program representatives upload a job/fellowship/residency description to ASHP's CareerPharm website (www.careerpharm.com), and candidates upload their résumé to the same site. This allows both parties to search programs or candidates and arrange to meet during the PPS. CareerPharm is open starting in September and closes at the end of January. Before and during the MCM, new opportunities are uploaded onto the website frequently.

As to the second question, whether you should sign up for the PPS if you are applying for a PGY1 residency, the answer is, it depends. Most PGY1 programs do not take part in PPS, but they will all be at the showcase. You should first identify PGY1 programs you are interested in and ask if they are participating in PPS. To inquire about this, send a professional email to the residency director. (See Sidebar 5-4 for email tips.) You can also look through the PPS directory on CareerPharm to see if a residency program you are interested in has a booth there. If you do not register for PPS in advance and discover while you're at the MCM that a program you're interested in is taking part, you can sign up on-site.

A major advantage to participating in PPS when searching for PGY1 residency programs is the 30-minute one-on-one interview with residency program representatives. No other students will be in the interview with you, so you don't need to compete for "face time." At the PPS, you can ask more questions and get more information than in the ASHP Residency Showcase. And the program representative gets to know *you* a little better in a less intense setting. Many students have mentioned to me (Monica) that they found PPS interviews helpful and were glad they had the opportunity to speak with program representatives in the venue. However, the PPS costs an additional fee in addition to the MCM registration fee. In 2012, the early registration was $55 and the late/on-site registration fee was $100. In addition, you can sign up for as many PPS interviews as you'd like, but it's best to avoid time slots during the Residency Showcase sessions.

At residency recruiting events, you should ask thoughtful questions about the program and take an active role in conversations—don't wait for people to talk with you.

— Ed Sheridan, Residency Director, Saint Joseph Regional Medical Center Pharmacy

Table 5-2 highlights some major differences between the two recruiting programs. A few tips to follow:

- If you are participating in PPS, post your résumé in September or October to give programs plenty of time to view your CV.

- Review postings for residencies on the CareerPharm website as early as possible and check the site often before the meeting.

- For the lowest price, purchase your registration before the early-bird deadline (usually about two weeks before the MCM).

- Sign up for interviews as soon as you know you're interested in a program to ensure there are slots open. You can sign up by contacting the program representative or sending a message via CareerPharm.

- Check your email box often during the meeting because programs may contact you to arrange an interview.

- Remember your meeting badge—required for entrance.

- Practice your interview questions and answers before attending your PPS sessions.

- After the PPS, send thank you cards to the people who interviewed you.

Table 5-2 | ASHP Residency Showcase versus Professional Placement Service

Residency Showcase	Professional Placement Service
Free for meeting participants	A fee is charged for all participants
Accessible to all meeting participants	Accessible only to registered participants
Showcase for most pharmacy residency programs	Typically for job, PGY2, and fellowship programs
Only 3 sessions, about 3 hours each	Open during the entire meeting
No appointments necessary	Appointments required
No interviews	In-person interviews offered
Program descriptions available prior to meeting	Program opportunities searchable prior to meeting
Talk with program residents and residency directors	Applicant résumés searchable prior to meeting
	Typically interview with program leadership

Conclusion

Probably the most important thing you can do to prepare for connecting with residency programs is to create a list of questions that target the information you need the most. When you meet with programs, whether at a school or at a state or national residency showcase, remember to keep your cool, act professionally, and use your time wisely—so you can determine whether the residency offers what you are seeking.

Reference

1. Caballero J, Clauson KA, Benavides S. *Get the Residency: ASHP's Guide to Residency Interviews and Preparation.* Bethesda, Md: American Society of Health-System Pharmacists; 2012:50–1.

Chapter 6

Preparing Your Application for a Pharmacy Residency

By Monica L. Miller and Deanna Kania

At this point in your residency search, you have learned about many different residency programs and have identified ones that seem a good fit for you. Now you need to decide which will make the "short list" for submitting your residency applications. What are some ways to determine your final choices? And which items will you need to include in your application packet?

This chapter discusses program selection and how to assemble your applications. It also reviews information about the Pharmacy Online Residency Centralized Application Service (PhORCAS).

> Think of the letter of intent as a way to tell the story of who you are.

Deciding Where to Apply

Selecting a residency program from those that interest you can be daunting, but it doesn't have to stress you out. You've already made a list of important attributes that you would like a residency program to possess (see Chapter 3). Now you can objectively compare the programs that pique your interest. One good way to examine programs more closely is to create a chart or spreadsheet that illustrates how well each prospective program fulfills your requirements.

Table 6-1 is an example of this type of comparison chart.

Table 6-1 | Sample Program Selection Chart

	Program A	Program B	Program C	Program D
Number of residents	3	1	10	6
Teaching certificate	No	Yes	Yes	Yes
Teaching hospital	Yes	No	Yes	Yes
College affiliation	Yes	No	Yes	Yes
Specialty residencies in internal medicine	No	No	Yes	Yes
Paid travel to meetings	Yes, 1	No	Yes, 1	Yes, 1
Liked program director	Yes	Yes	Yes	Yes
Had positive interactions with the residents	Yes	Yes	Yes	Yes
Have received emails back from my initial inquiry	Yes	Yes	Yes	Yes

To create your own chart, first list the factors that are most important to you in a residency (strategies to identify these factors are discussed in Chapter 3). The candidate who created this sample chart is looking for a larger program at a teaching hospital with a teaching certificate offered, among other items. She also added categories for nonobjective criteria, such as how well she felt she connected with the programs' directors. For some, taking these "gut" feelings into account is an important part of the decision-making process.

Then, list the programs you are considering and check whether each meets or doesn't meet your criteria. In the sample chart, programs A, C, and D have all the elements this candidate considered to be priorities. Program B was missing some key components that interested her, but it probably made her short list because she enjoyed meeting and interacting with the residency program director and current residents.

Of course, this candidate—and you—will have to decide how much weight to give each factor on the list and then determine the final score for each program. After completing the comparison process, you should have a good idea of the residencies you'll consider.

What to Include in a Residency Application

What items are included in a residency application? Most programs require you to submit your transcripts, a letter of intent, an up-to-date curriculum vitae(CV) (you learned how to create and polish your CV in Chapter 4), and three letters of recommendation. Some programs may ask for other materials, such as a supplemental application form from you or a form from the people writing your letters of recommendation.

Letter of Intent

A letter of intent, or cover letter, conveys your specific areas of interest to a program and also demonstrates your passion for pharmacy. A well-crafted letter can differentiate you from other candidates and may even be a factor in whether you move on to the interview phase of the application process.

Think of the letter as a way to tell the story of who you are. Using a professional approach, you convey your interests, your goals, and what you hope to achieve through your residency. You also include personal examples of how you've gained a skill set that is unique to you. These details tell more about you as a person than your CV does on its own. For example, when I (Monica) was writing my letters of intent, I wanted to make sure the readers knew I had begun developing leadership and communication skills, so I included examples of my role as a student officer in a professional organization.

Many programs want a one-page letter of intent, including addresses and signatures, so stick to that length unless you check to be sure they will accept two pages. The letter should never be more than two pages long, and typically it contains three to four paragraphs that provide an opening statement of interest, specific reasons why the residency program appeals to you, your qualifications, and a closing statement. Your letter of intent should answer the following questions:

- Why are you interested in this particular residency?

- What are your professional goals?

- How does this residency help you achieve those goals?

- What relevant skills and experiences do you bring to the program?

Your letter of intent should reflect and elaborate on items your CV contains. For example, you might say, "I was able to develop my communication skills by giving presentations to prospective members and editing the monthly newsletter of the XYZ Student Organization." This organization should then be listed on your CV.

> Letters of recommendation are strongest when they contain specific information about you.

Before beginning your draft, look at templates for letters of intent, available online, and ask classmates, colleagues, or your school's resource personnel to share letters with you that they consider good examples. Make sure you do not plagiarize the content of sample letters you review.

After you have drafted your letter, ask a few trusted readers, such as mentors or professors, to review it and suggest ways you can make it more effective. Proofread carefully to catch grammatical and spelling errors, and ask others to check your letter for typos you might have missed, flow of ideas, and overall content. Examples of a good letter of intent and a poor one appear at the end of this chapter. See Sidebar 6-1 for a summary of tips.

Sidebar 6-1. Tips for Letters of Intent

- Check grammar and spelling.

- Tell a story; make people excited about you by helping them see your strengths, accomplishments, and potential.

- Be articulate and professional.

- Avoid using generic phrases and clichés.

- Have the letter reviewed by an outside person.

- Convey a sense of confidence.

- Do not copy an example letter verbatim; follow it loosely as a guide, but use your own words and phrases.

Letters of Recommendation

Most residency application packages require you to submit three letters of recommendation—from your preceptors, professors, employers, or other mentors. These letters help program directors learn more about you from people who have worked with you or with whom you have shared classroom or volunteer experiences.

Letters of recommendation are strongest when they contain specific information about you. When you request one, it's best to ask people who know you well, with whom you have had substantive, positive interactions. Be sure to ask if these people are comfortable accepting the task before sending them specific information about what you need.

To make writing the letters as convenient and easy as possible for them, refer to the suggestions in Sidebar 6-2. And of course, remember that these people are doing you a favor. Thank them in advance for helping you, and also write a note expressing your appreciation.

Sidebar 6-2. Tips for Great Letters of Recommendation

- When you request a letter from someone, give him or her plenty of lead time—at least one month before the letter is due.

- Create a package of information to share with letter writers. For each program, include your CV, the program director's name and titles, the practice setting, what attracted you to the program, and the program's address and application deadline.

- Consider providing suggestions for information to include if the person has not written many recommendation letters, or if he or she requests it. Ideas such as the following can provide direction:

  ○ How long has the letter writer known you, and in what capacity?

  ○ What does he or she see as your strengths, and how might they be applied in the program that you are targeting?

  ○ What skills and experiences do you possess that will be valuable to the program?

  ○ In what areas can you improve?

  ○ What is his or her overall recommendation?

Pharmacy Online Residency Centralized Application Service (PhORCAS)

PhORCAS is an online tool that captures all the pieces of your residency application in a centralized location, similar to PharmCAS. This tool helps both applicants and programs track the items in your residency application packet and streamlines the application process. For instance, if the residency programs you are interested in use PhORCAS, you can have your letters of recommendation sent to them electronically.

Sidebar 6-3 details some of the ways PhORCAS can be helpful to candidates and pharmacy programs. More information can be found at www.ashp.org.

Sidebar 6-3. Advantages of Using PhORCAS

PhORCAS provides services to residency applicants and to the programs themselves.

Advantages to Applicants
- Online submissions disseminated to multiple programs.

- Electronic tracking and notification of application process.

- Reduced applicant paperwork.

- Flexibility to customize.

- Consolidation of the National Matching Service and PhORCAS registration.

- System available for a post-match process.

Advantages to Residency Program
- Decreased administrative burden.

- Electronic tracking of application process.

- Prescreening of applicant eligibility.

- Candidates sorted by different criteria.

- Flexibility if program wishes to change requirements.

- System available for a post-match process.

Submitting Your Applications

As the applicant pool increases and residency programs become more competitive, candidates are beginning to apply to more programs. Each person is different—I've (Monica) known some who apply to only one program, and some who've applied to as many as 12, but the typical number of applications people submit is five to 10.

It's an individual decision, based on your particular circumstances. If you want to stay in a particular geographic region, you will have to choose from a more limited pool of programs. Cost may also become an issue, because fees will increase along with the number of programs you select.

In general, you should apply to programs that mean the most to you—the ones that, if program representative offered you an interview, you would be thrilled to accept.

After you submit your application, it's a good idea to contact the program and check to see that they have received all your materials, even if the program is using the PhORCAS system. Once your application is complete, the waiting game begins. You will wait to be contacted by a program representative, typically in January, who will either tell you that you've been offered an interview or say that, unfortunately, you did not receive an interview offer.

When I (Monica) was going through the application process, I sent my package of material to programs by overnight delivery. A few days later I'd follow up to ensure that everything was received. Even with the new electronic application process, it is still a good idea to follow up because it's your responsibility to get all the application pieces into the program's hands. I had to check on the transcripts and letters of recommendation a few times because the transcripts took longer to be sent than I'd expected, and a few of my recommenders needed reminders about sending in their letters.

Conclusion

It can be a challenge to narrow down the list of residency programs before submitting applications. Compare and contrast programs carefully so that you apply only to those that truly interest you. When submitting an application, ensure that you have an up-to-date CV, well-written letter of intent, and three glowing letters of recommendation. Last of all, follow up with the residency programs to make sure your application is complete.

Letters of Intent Examples

Good Letter: Well written and articulate. It clearly states why the candidate is interested in this residency program, expresses what experiences this person will bring to the program, and states some of the candidate's professional goals. It also highlights the writer's strengths and expresses confidence but not arrogance.

Poor Letter: Although the letter has some positive aspects, such as good examples included, it is wordy and has grammatical and spelling mistakes. It doesn't state what the writer's future plans and goals are and doesn't answer the question, "How will this program help you reach your goals?" In addition, it sounds somewhat generic when talking about the hospital setting. It also lacks important details, such as the letter writer's contact information.

Good Letter of Intent

Name
Address, City, ST Zip
Phone # - email address
Date

Residency Director Name, PharmD
Orange City VAMC Department of Pharmacy
Street, City, ST Zip

Dear Dr. Residency Director,

I am writing to express my interest in the PGY1 Pharmacy Practice Residency Program at Oblong VA Medical Center. After speaking with you and your residents at the ASHP Midyear Clinical Meeting, I consider your residency program an ideal fit for my professional goals. The structure of your program, with its variety of elective opportunities, teaching certification, and longitudinal responsibilities, offers a diverse and comprehensive experience. I have a strong appreciation for the Veterans Affairs and am passionate about helping those who have served our country.

I appreciate the long-term care and follow-up involved in the ambulatory care practice, which allows for the opportunity to develop a continuum of care with patients. The residency program at Oblong VA fulfills all of my interests, including longitudinal ambulatory care clinics and strong academia involvement. It will help me expand and refine my clinical knowledge in the ever-changing health care environment while allowing me to work in a setting that interests me. My short-term goals include pursuing a PGY2 in ambulatory care and becoming a Board Certified Pharmacotherapy Specialist with involvement in academia and student preceptorship. My long-term goal is to help others become advocates for their own health and provide patient education that allows them to achieve a thorough understanding of their health and medications.

Throughout the past four years, I have been actively involved in pharmacy organizations and have worked as a pharmacy technician, which has allowed me ample opportunities to interact with patients. As chair of my college's APhA-ASP Operation Immunization, I organized over 30 projects and 150 events in one school year, which involved more than 200 student pharmacists. As secretary of Class Council and Phi Lambda Sigma, I've been recognized by my peers for my excellent communication skills. By working in the Medication Therapy Management Clinic at Circle Medical Center, I have gained an understanding of various patient educational tools and practices to help manage complex medication regimens. These experiences have given me an interest in and appreciation for disease state management and patient education. I've also served as a peer mentor and organized patient education projects and presentations, through which I have developed an interest in academia, which I'd like to pursue in your teaching certificate program. The exciting opportunities your institution provides for my interests in academia and pharmacy practice will allow me to pursue my long-term goals.

My leadership experience, communication skills, personality, and strong work ethic will allow me to succeed in your PGY1 residency and career. Enclosed are my application requirements for your review. Thank you for your time and consideration. I look forward to speaking with you soon.

Sincerely,

My Name, PharmD Candidate
Town Center College of Pharmacy

Poor Letter of Intent

*No address or contact information
provided from the letter writer*

Attn: Residency Director's Name
VA Medical Center
Address
City, ST Zip

Dear Dr. Preceptor,   *Spelling error*

I am writing this letter to express my interest in your post-graduate year one (PGY-1) pharmacy
program. After looking through the ACHP Residency Directory posting and further researching your
hospital through materials emailed to me, I am greatly excited about the opportunities your
program can offer me.

No period at the end of the sentence   *Spelling error*

The VA PGY-1 residency program has many aspects that are appealing to me and suit my
interests. Among these include a diversified experience in hospital pharmacy with rotations ranging
from internal medicine to drug information Of special interest tome is the wide opportunity provided
in ambulatory care through your pharmacist-run clinics and specialty ambulatory care clinics as
well as the chance and preference to teach future pharmacists. Most of all, I look forward to
expanding my clinical experience in many areas in order to become a better practitioner as well as
fine-tuning my skills for further specialization. I am certain thi residency will provide me with the
knowledge and clinical expertise that I need to incorporate into my career and further enhance the
profession of pharmacy. After completing residency, I hope to practice in an ambulatory focused
setting such as yours since it provides me with the direct patient care in a hospital environment that
I desire and am most excited about.

Spelling error

I believe I would be an excellent fit for your program. I am a hard-working individual with dedication
and passion for my work. For me, the enthusiasm for pharmacy came early in my life when I
learned how fascinating the interplay between science and the body can be. I was able to pursue
this interest early on in large part due to my admission into a dual acceptance program during high
school. Additionally, my work experience in a retail environment has taught me lessons in
interpersonal skills and direct patient care that are applicable to any environment. Furthermore,
anticoagulation management at my current rotation at Giraffe Hospital has especially sparked my
interest while pharmaceutical knowledge and have provided me with valuable clinical experience
that I look forward to implementing and perfecting through your residency program.

Grammar mistake

Sincerely,   *There is no closing paragraph*

Name
PharmD Candidate
Town University College of Pharmacy

Chapter 7

The Residency Interview

By Monica L. Miller and Deanna Kania

Interviewing with a residency program is an exciting milestone in your residency search. Fewer candidates are reaching the interview stage these days because of the competition for residency positions. So if you have interviews scheduled, first, celebrate your accomplishment! And next, determine what you need to do to be well prepared, so that you can make the most of the interview experience.

This chapter provides an overview of the residency interview and highlights strategies you can use to get ready for your time in the spotlight. The better prepared you are, the more confident and relaxed you will be—and the greater your chance of success.

My interview experiences were all very different. One site required a written pharmacology exam and interviews with entire inpatient teams of 10 pharmacists. Another site started out with a casual pizza lunch. You may have an itinerary ahead of time, but you won't know what the experience will be like until you walk in the door. Be ready for the most rigorous possible experience, and you will be pleasantly relieved if it's more casual.

—Caity Frail

Residency Interview Purpose

The residency interview is a critical step toward obtaining a residency program. Nothing can replace actually being at the site, interacting with the people, and observing the work environment. Programs use the interview process to get to know candidates on a more personal level, assess how they fit with the program and staff, and determine how to rank each person among all the contenders for residency slots. During the interview, candidates get to examine the program and location closely, observe the overall workflow, meet people, and see how everyone relates with each other. They also learn more about the attributes of the city and geographical area.

As much as programs are looking for the "right fit" among candidates, you, too, are looking for the program that's the right fit for you, and the interview process will help you make that determination.

Overview of a Residency Interview

Residency program interviews may last anywhere from a half day to a full day or more. Some programs require candidates to deliver a presentation; others want candidates to display their clinical skills by solving a pharmacotherapy case, writing a progress note, answering a drug information question, or leading a journal club. Some interviews may include a meal, such as dinner the night before or breakfast or lunch on the actual day. All programs allow for interview sessions with preceptors, current residents, pharmacy staff, and the residency directors as well as a tour of the facility. Amanda Slinde recalls, "There were several rounds of interviews with different clinical pharmacists, along with the residency director, pharmacy managers, and current residents. In some cases, there was a Q and A session with the current residents."

Says John Hertig, "All of my interviews lasted a full day. We would start off the morning by going over the general aspects of the program. I would then meet various pharmacy and hospital staff who asked focused questions specific to each of their areas, and I was allowed to ask questions throughout the day. I would encourage candidates to ask intelligent questions because it demonstrates interest, engagement, and a willingness to dig deeper."

Some programs conduct their interviews using a panel of health care professionals. Some use a group interview format, where you may be one of several candidates answering questions together in one room.

Almost all programs include a resident interview session in which you ask the current resident questions about his or her year so far and probe for insights into the program from the resident's perspective. Often this is a group interview, attended by many candidates at once. Try not to overpower the session or cut people off, but be assertive enough to ask and answer questions. Although the session may feel relaxed, remember that it is still an interview. Most likely, the resident will provide feedback about you to the program personnel to help them rank the candidates.

Your "interview" encompasses all of your encounters, from the time you arrive in the city where the program is located until the time you leave. Wherever you are—traveling to the interview site, in the lobby of the building, at lunch, or during your facility tour—you are being evaluated, so your behavior should always be focused and professional.

"You have to be 'on' the whole time," says Ashley Crumby. "You are constantly in the company of someone associated with the residency program, so there really is no down time until the interview is over. Even when you are just with the residents and they tell you it is okay to speak freely, you have to remember to be cautious."

Getting Ready for Interview Season

Your residency interviews will be scheduled during the winter, typically in January and February of your final year in pharmacy school. During the months leading up to interview season, you should make preparations to help the interview process go more smoothly.

First get to know yourself well—what are you looking for in a residency program? What are your goals? You will have to articulate the answers during the residency interview.

Anticipate the costs involved in interviewing and budget for them. Attending networking events and job fairs, submitting applications, and traveling to residency interviews all involve significant fees that vary depending on how many interviews you take part in and how far away they are. Sidebar 7-1 outlines items you will want to consider.

Knowing that you will have to dress professionally for networking events and interviews, you should shop for your business attire in advance. Sidebar 7-2 contains some suggestions for appropriate dress for networking events and interviews.

Sidebar 7-1. Budgeting for Your Residency Search

Here are some expenses you should consider as you plan for your residency search:

- Midyear networking events and job fairs.
  - Meeting registration fees.
  - Hotel accommodations.
  - Travel costs (airfare or gas, plus transportation during the meetings).
  - Meals (if not provided).
- Registration fee for the American Society of Health-System Pharmacists (ASHP) Professional Placement Service (optional).
- Business cards and curriculum vitae (CV) (design and printing).
- Registration fee for the ASHP Resident Matching Program.
- Registration fee for Pharmacy Online Residency Centralized Application Service (PhORCAS), if applicable.
- Resident interviews.
  - Hotel accommodations.
  - Travel costs (airfare or gas, plus transportation during the meetings).
  - Meals (if not provided).
- Business attire (interview suit and accessories).
- Thank-you notes and postage.

Getting Ready for Your Interview

Getting ready for your residency interview may be the most important step in the entire process. Being well prepared—researching residency programs, thinking about interview questions, reflecting on your answers beforehand, and practicing your communication skills—will help you feel more comfortable during the interview and allow you to demonstrate your interest in the program.

Sidebar 7-2. Professional Attire for Interviewing

When you are meeting representatives of professional programs, it's vital to present yourself as professional. Your appearance is what people notice first.

- Avoid strong perfumes or colognes.

- Remove any facial and oral cavity piercings.

- Wear well-fitting, appropriate attire. Business suits are recommended for both men and women. (Have them tailored to fit you properly.)

- Avoid clashing colors in your attire.

- Wear appropriate shoes. You will walk a lot during the day—so choose a pair that is comfortable yet professional, and make sure your shoes look new and polished.

Women:
- Avoid very high heels.

- Wear makeup to the interview, but don't overdo it.

- Your suit can include either a skirt or slacks.

- Wear a classic shirt that is not cut too low.

Men:
- Invest in a well-fitted suit and a good tie/shirt combination.

- Wear black or blue socks depending on the color of your suit—no white socks with your dress shoes.

You want to be your best during the interview, and preparation will allow you to shine. Here are some things to consider before each of your interviews.

Learn about the Program
The more information you learn about each program in advance, the better you can articulate what makes the program interesting to you and why you are a good fit. You'll be able to ask more insightful, targeted questions.

- Review the residency's website and promotional materials.

- Read the mission, vision, and values statements.

- Research the interviewers you'll be seeing, particularly the residency director, so you can ask questions about them and their experiences, if time allows.

  ○ Do a search on PubMed, the online database that covers journals and abstracts in biomedicine and health, to see what each interviewer has published.

  ○ Identify the interviewer's practice setting and area of expertise, such as internal medicine, ambulatory care, intensive care unit, etc.

  ○ If possible, identify which pharmacy school the interviewer went to and the residency program he or she completed.

> Programs use the interview process to get to know candidates on a more personal level, assess how they fit with the program and staff, and determine how to rank each person among all the contenders.

Be Prepared for Questions about You

Representatives from residency programs will want to determine your level of passion for the pharmacy profession, your motivation for seeking residency training, your long-term career goals, and your strengths and weaknesses. Before sitting down with an interviewer, reflecting on—and practicing—answers to commonly asked questions will allow you to collect your thoughts and express yourself clearly. When practicing your answers, write down experiences that have helped shape you as a practitioner. Also, think about times when you have had an impact on patient care.

Interviews are stressful, and if you're like me (Monica), you always think of the perfect answer to a question after you've left the interview room. To get over this, I started doing practice interviews. I wrote down key points I wanted the interviewer to know about me, and I reread this list several times to imprint it on my mind—including right before the interview. That way, good examples came easily when I was answering questions, and I was able to leave interviewers with things I wanted them to remember about me.

When answering interview questions, keep the focus on your professional development. Use examples from pharmacy school or rotations that relate to questions being asked. For example, a common question is, "Can you tell me about yourself?" Your answer should be a two-minute summary that is work and education-related, not your life story or a review of your hobbies.

Interviewers also like to ask, "What are some of your nonprofessional goals?" Although it's tempting to answer with statements such as, "To get married," or "To have a family in the next few years," we encourage you to think of an answer that has nothing to do with family or marital status, no matter how important these things are to you. Instead, provide insights into your personality and your pursuits outside of pharmacy, such as hobbies and sports. Such examples will set you apart because they are unique to you. For example, we've heard candidates say, "I want to train for a marathon," "I want to get my scuba certification," and "I want to travel to all 50 states." These replies fleshed out the candidates and made them seem like people with a zest for life.

"Can you tell me some of your weaknesses?" another common question, can catch you off guard if you don't think it through in advance. We all have weaknesses, but it's good to present something that the residency will help you improve—and something that is not essential to your overall success as a pharmacist. For example, you could say, "I get nervous when giving group presentations. This residency will give me the opportunity to practice and grow more comfortable."

Some sample questions for candidates appear in Sidebar 7-3.

Occasionally you may encounter an unusual question that seems to have little to do with pharmacy. Isabel Hagedorn says her interviewers asked, "If you were a car, what make, model, and year would you be?" and, "If you were a piece of fruit, what would you be and why?" In cases like this, adds Ashley Crumby, "Sometimes the answer may not even matter; they may only be interested in how you handle the question."

Sidebar 7-3. Sample Questions for Interview Candidates

Here are some typical questions you may be asked during your residency interview.

- Can you tell me about yourself?
- Why did you choose pharmacy as a career?
- Why do you want to do a residency?
- Why are you interested in this particular program?
- Where do you see yourself in five years?
- What are your overall career goals?
- How can you contribute to this organization?
- What would you change about your pharmacy school?
- What was your favorite clinical rotation, and why?
- What was your least favorite clinical rotation, and why?
- What are your strengths and weaknesses? What is your plan for overcoming your weaknesses?
- Describe a current issue in pharmacy today. How will it impact your future clinical practice?
- Describe a time when you received constructive criticism. How did it change you and your behavior?
- What do you like to do in your spare time?
- Describe a time when your time management skills were tested. What new things did you learn?
- What makes you angry?
- What do you worry about?
- What motivates you?
- Who is your mentor and why?
- Can you describe an event in your life that has forever changed you as a future clinical pharmacist?
- Can you describe yourself in three words?
- What makes you the most qualified candidate for this position?

"Tell Me When" Requests

Interviewers may also ask about how you reacted in certain circumstances. "Tell me about a time when…" requests are sometimes based on ideas that occur to residency personnel when they read your CV, but they can also be more general and relate to other areas of your life. Examples might include times when you have given great clinical recommendations, dealt with conflicts, or provided leadership in difficult situations. Examples of these types of requests appear in Sidebar 7-4.

Rehearsing relevant stories ahead of time can make for a smoother presentation and increase your confidence. When I (Monica) was preparing for interviews, I wrote down answers to all the potential "tell me about a time when" requests I could think of. During one residency interview I was asked, "Tell me a time when you experienced conflict. How did you deal with it?" I'd recently had an issue arise between me and a fellow student. I was able to briefly describe the situation and what we did to resolve it in a "win-win" fashion. You should always answer "tell me about a time" requests concisely, and be specific about what you did. Also, avoid painting the other person in the conflict in a negative light. Just state facts.

Review Your CV

Interviewers may use your CV to generate questions during your interview, so you should refamiliarize yourself with the information you included. Be able to discuss all items on your CV in detail such as your presentations, topic discussions, journal clubs, projects, posters, and activities. Tap the information in your CV to highlight your accomplishments and demonstrate that you are just as impressive in person as you are on paper.

Participate in Practice Interviews

Rehearsing for your interview beforehand can be helpful for several reasons. During practice sessions, you can think out loud and refine your answers until you formulate a concise and effective response. If you stumble, you can start again. Revisit the same question until your answer feels natural. ("Practice how you'd answer common questions—a lot!" urges Ashley Johns.)

Doing a "dry run" can make you feel more poised during the interview, because the questions you're asked will be somewhat familiar to you. During practice sessions you can get advice on your presentation skills—the pace and volume of your speech, whether you fidget or use distracting fillers such as "um" or "you know," and how effectively you make eye contact.

Sidebar 7-4. Sample "Tell Me When" Requests

The following are examples of requests that require you to reflect on your experiences and discuss how you handled a situation. During your pharmacy interview, you may be asked the following:

- Describe a situation in which you had to use your communication skills in presenting complex information. How did you determine whether your message was received?

- Share with me an example of an important personal goal that you set, and explain how you accomplished it.

- Lead me through a decision-making process on a major project you've completed.

- Describe a time in which you used persuasion to reach consensus on your point of view.

- Have you ever had many different tasks given to you at the same time? How did you manage these?

- Give an example of a time when you had too many things on your plate and, as a result, something did not go well or as planned. What did you learn?

- Describe a time in which you dealt with an angry coworker or customer. What was the conflict and how was it resolved?

- Tell me about a time that you had to go "above and beyond the call of duty."

- Give an example of a time you had to make a difficult decision.

- Discuss a situation where you made a mistake and you had to resolve the issue.

- Describe a time when you had to make an unpopular decision.

Some colleges of pharmacy and professional organizations offer practice interview sessions to help you gain experience and get constructive feedback. You can also conduct a mock interview with friends, relatives, or coworkers, watch yourself in a mirror, or videotape yourself to assess how well you come across.

Polish Your Presentation

If giving a presentation is part of your residency interview, make sure it is excellent in every way. Your residency program audience is assessing the clinical information you include, your communication skills, and your poise under pressure.

> You want to be your best during the interview, and preparation will allow you to shine.

- Select a presentation you have given before, to help reduce your stress and allow you to focus on polishing the presentation rather than creating new material. You might use a case presentation from a rotation or a research presentation about a project you're working on.

- Practice giving the presentation several times before your interview.

- Have a preceptor or mentor review your PowerPoint slides.

- Bring a copy of your presentation on a flash drive and have it stored on a cloud hosting site, such as Dropbox, so you have more than one way of accessing it in case of a technology failure.

- Bring notes for yourself, if you need them.

- Make sure your presentation fulfills the requirements of the program.

- Keep the presentation length to the designated time frame.

- Practice your transitions to cut out filler words such as "um," "like," and "so."

Preparations for Interview Day

You may feel excited or nervous about your interview, and anticipating ways to make the day go more smoothly can be helpful.

First, allow plenty of time to travel to the interview site. Schedule flights or train trips to arrive the day before your interview in case of bad weather or delays—especially because residency interviews are conducted during the winter. Include your essential clothing and toiletries in your carry-on luggage. Korby Lathrop recalls this travel mishap: "The airline misplaced my bag for a few days. Luckily I had carried on a suit."

If you're driving from your hotel or home city, plan enough travel time to allow for traffic or other issues. Make sure you have good directions and that you know where to park and where to go once inside the facility.

Plan to arrive at the interview site a half hour early, to give yourself ample time to collect yourself, check your appearance, and make sure you have all the materials you need. Arrive in the reception area or meeting room five minutes early (but not sooner, because interviewers may have other items on their schedule).

Here are a few items you may want to bring with you:

- Program contact information.

- A pad and pen.

- Your list of questions for interviewers.

- Your notes about the program and preceptors.

- Your notes about yourself—including things you want to be sure to mention.

- Copies of articles, posters, or portfolios of your work.

- Your presentation, if applicable (on your laptop, a flash drive, or Internet site such as Dropbox).

- A hard copy of your PowerPoint slides.

- A copy of your itinerary.

- A bottle of water, because you will talk a lot throughout the day.

- Your cell phone in case someone from the program needs to reach you—but turn it off or put it on "silent" when you get to the interview.

No matter how well you plan ahead, you might encounter a situation out of your control, such as a traffic accident or delayed flight. Ask your contacts at the residency program for the best way to contact them in case of an emergency.

Sonia Vainrub "missed a plane and was unable to get another flight out to my interview on the upcoming day. It was terrible. I had to call the program director (who was going to be picking me up at the airport) to apologize. After some emailing back and forth over the next few days, she rescheduled me."

Tips for a Successful Interview

A common piece of advice for people going into interviews is, "Be yourself." But that's a little simplistic. You certainly want to be honest and genuine, but an interview is not a typical situation for most of us. It's a formal professional opportunity, so you should tailor your behavior and use communication strategies to present yourself in the most effective and flattering way. Here are some ideas.

Smile

We start with this point because it's so important to come across as personable and positive. Smiling projects excitement and makes others feel you are happy to be at the interview. Smiling is a good icebreaker; people seem approachable when they smile. There's even psychological evidence that smiling can make you feel more relaxed. So even though you're nervous, remember to smile.

By the end of the day, your face should hurt from smiling so much. We've seen interviews where the candidate didn't smile at all, and afterwards, the program personnel concluded, "I guess they aren't excited about our program."

Dress Professionally

Whether you like it or not, the first impression you make has a lot to do with your appearance. Stand out for your professional attributes, not for what you are wearing. People remember poorly dressed candidates. Refer to Sidebar 7-2 for tips.

Ask Questions

Asking thoughtful questions of program representatives is one of the most important ways you can indicate your interest in their residency. From the research you have done about the organization and its staff, develop a list specific to their program. These questions may relate to opportunities within the program, job duties, coming changes, growth potential, and experiences the staff have had in their particular positions.

You've already seen some sample questions for program representatives in Chapter 5. Additional ones to consider are included in Sidebar 7-5.

Having questions prepared demonstrates your knowledge of, and enthusiasm for, the residency. It's also an opportunity to get additional information to determine if the program is the best one for you. As we've mentioned, you and the program representatives are really interviewing each other to see if you are a good fit.

Ask questions during each phase of your interview, even if you ask the same thing more than once. Sometimes hearing different people's perspectives on topics such as changes coming up in the residency program can be instructive.

It can be especially helpful to question current residents about their experiences in the program. They may provide insights and information you won't find on an organization's website. Listen carefully to their answers, paraphrase their responses, and ask follow-up questions if possible.

Be a Good Listener

You will be asked a lot of questions during the course of the interview day. Listen carefully, ask for clarification if you do not understand the question, and do not start answering until the questioner has stopped speaking. Then answer completely. It's okay to take a few seconds to formulate your answer.

You'll be asked some questions you haven't prepared for. When this happens, do your best to answer each question, and then move on. Let the interviewer guide the questions—don't try to take control.

**Sidebar 7-5. Sample Questions to Ask During Your
             Residency Interview**

Here are some questions you may want to consider asking the program director
or preceptors:

- Over the past few years, where have your residency candidates gone upon
  graduation?

- What changes are anticipated for the residency program over the next three
  to five years?

- What have been the greatest accomplishments for the residency program in
  the past three to five years?

- What makes a successful resident?

- What qualities do you desire in a residency candidate?

- Will there be opportunities for involvement in the residency accreditation
  process?

- How does this program demonstrate a commitment to the outcomes of the
  residents?

- What are the teaching opportunities available in this program—both didactic
  and experiential? (precepting)

- What research projects are your clinical staff currently conducting?

- Do residents have opportunities to collaborate on existing research?

- What opportunities exist for publishing?

- Outside of the ASHP Midyear Clinical Meeting, are residents encouraged to
  attend local, regional, or other national conferences?

- If I were marketing the services of this hospital or pharmacy, what would be
  included in the ad?

- What makes your program different from other programs?

- What are your favorite aspects of your job? What are your least favorite?

continued on page 124

123

Sidebar 7-5. Sample Questions to Ask During Your Residency Interview, *continued*

- Who are the faculty at your site and what are their interests? (if relevant)
- Would you please describe the evaluation process for your residents?
- How do you incorporate the teaching roles of direct instruction, modeling, coaching, and facilitating into each of your learning experiences?
- What medication therapy management privileges do your pharmacists have?
- What impact does pharmacy have on managing or creating the formulary?
- What are the elective rotation or learning experiences available at this site?

Here are some questions you may want to consider asking the residents in the program:

- What are the salary and health insurance coverage like?
- What is a typical week like on an inpatient rotation? On an outpatient rotation? On a staffing weekend? On an on-call night?
- Would you please discuss your current research projects?
- Would you tell me about your relationship with the program directors, the preceptors, your mentor, and your project advisor?
- What are your plans upon the completion of this residency?
- How do you market this program to local students?
- In what area of your job do you feel you learn the most?
- What has been your biggest challenge during this residency year?
- What is it like living in this city?
- Overall, are you happy with your match?

If you're truly listening, maintaining eye contact and an interested expression will come naturally. Nod and gesture when appropriate to engage with the interviewer and reinforce that you are absorbing what is being said. Also, listen carefully to the answers people give to your questions. Not only are they providing important information for your eventual residency decision, but their response can guide your next question.

Project Confidence and Enthusiasm

Show that you are a confident person. As you enter a room, stand tall, relax your shoulders, and keep your right hand free to give a firm handshake. When you're sitting down, keep your back straight and lean slightly forward, toward the interviewer.

Do not shrink when asked a tough question; instead, draw on your preparation to answer with confidence. Remind yourself that you are a great candidate. If you come across as confident, residency personnel will start developing confidence in you, as well.

Express enthusiasm throughout the interview process through statements such as, "I like this program because...," or "I really respect this organization and its mission." Convey the ways that your attributes will contribute to the program's strengths. At the same time—and this sounds contradictory—don't be "over the top" in your enthusiasm. It's a fine line. If you overdo it, you may seem fake and leave a poor impression. During your practice interviews, try to polish how you come across so you project the right amount of enthusiasm.

Highlight Your Accomplishments

Sometimes speaking about your skills and accomplishments feels uncomfortable. You may worry that you're bragging or being egotistical. But during an interview, it's absolutely appropriate to explain why you feel you are a good candidate, or to tell a story that highlights something you do well.

Getting support ahead of time can make it easier to talk about yourself. "I usually needed a pep talk before each interview," says Carolyn Jung. "I have a tough time letting people see who I am in an interview, and I always worry about that beforehand. Talking to someone who knows me well helps me to remember why I am a good candidate for the job and what I can say or do to show that."

Remind yourself that interviewers expect you to explain why you will be an asset to their program. Otherwise, why would you seek a position with them?

Have a Positive Attitude and Exhibit Professionalism

It's possible that you will be asked about an experience that was challenging for you. Even if you feel that someone was unfair to you, or that a situation did not go well because of someone else's error, cast a positive light on the experience by describing how you learned from it. Blaming others or speaking disrespectfully about a rotation or preceptor will reflect poorly on you; people may assume that you might be disrespectful or talk behind their back, too.

Avoid negative words or phrases, even during questions about a negative experience. Keep your comments honest, but with a positive spin. In addition, avoid sabotaging yourself with irritating habits such as tapping a pen, twirling hair, biting nails, picking at split ends, using slang, or peppering your speech with verbal tics such as "like," "you know," "so, yeah," and "stuff like that."

It's important to remember that not only are they interviewing you, you're interviewing them. You need to be yourself to know whether you'll fit with the pharmacy team.

These are the people you'll be spending the next year plus of your life with. Don't try to answer questions based on what you think they want to hear—interviewers see right through that.

—Isabel Hagedorn

Wrap Up Each Session Effectively

After each individual session in your interview, thank the people who spoke with you and restate your interest in the program. At the end of the day, when the interview is wrapping up, reemphasize your enthusiasm to the program director and other representatives. Make sure people know that you are excited about the program, happy to have visited, and appreciative of the opportunity to talk with them.

Telephone Interviews

Some programs conduct telephone interviews as part of the application screening process or during the "Scramble," which is discussed in Chapter 8. Phone interviews are short interactions but highly important, so take them seriously. See Sidebar 7-6 for tips on effective phone interviews.

Sidebar 7-6. Tips for Telephone Interviews

If you need to participate in an interview over the telephone, follow the tips below.

Do
- Know how much time is being allocated to the phone interview and plan accordingly. If it's scheduled for one hour, block off a full hour in your day when you will be able to focus only on the interview.

- Conduct the interview at home so you can focus without work or school interruptions.

- Keep the background quiet. Avoid noise from children, pets, music, the dishwasher, or the TV.

- Answer the phone professionally. Saying "Hello, this is Monica" allows the interviewer to know that he or she has reached the correct person, and it starts the interview off on a good note.

- Smile. It sounds odd, but if you smile while conducting a telephone interview, the interviewer will hear it in your voice.

- Dress for the interview even though the interviewer can't see you. It puts you in a professional frame of mind.

- Do your research about the program. Prepare thoughtful questions, just as you would for an onsite interview, and create a sheet of points you want to make.

- Jot notes during the interview using pen and paper. Typing on your computer can be a distraction to the interviewer.

- Have a copy of your CV in front of you so you can refer to it if necessary.

- Speak slowly and enunciate.

- Be concise with your answers and avoid rambling. Take several seconds to think about your reply before speaking.

- Keep a glass of water handy in case your throat gets dry.

continued on page 128

Sidebar 7-6. Tips for Telephone Interviews, *continued*

Don't

- Answer another incoming call or text.

- Surf the web or check your emails.

- Eat, chew gum, or smoke.

- Interrupt the interviewer. Let him or her finish the question before you start talking.

- Conduct the interview while driving or walking. It's unsafe and exposes the interviewer to distracting noise from traffic and your surroundings.

Interviewing with Programs You Know

Sometimes you will schedule an interview with a residency program with which you're already familiar. You may have done a rotation or a school project there, so your interviewers may be people you know. In addition, you may already have a good deal of information about the facility.

The most important thing to remember in this situation is to conduct yourself professionally, as you would in any interview. This interview is not informal, no matter how well you know the people or the place. Be prepared and respectful, answer questions thoughtfully, and explain why you have enjoyed working within the program.

Even if your performance during your rotation has been exemplary and you have expressed your interest to the program representatives, they are comparing your behavior with that of other candidates. Show them that you appreciate their time and effort and use good judgment by valuing the opportunity to interview with them.

Interviewing If You're Shy or Introverted

Many great pharmacy residency candidates struggle to stand out because they are soft spoken or have reserved personalities. Don't let shyness get in the way of your interview. You may worry, "What if I don't have anything to say?" "Will my answers be too short?" "What if I can't get a word in edgewise?" Practice, as we've discussed many times in this chapter, is the best way to overcome these issues. The tips below relate to different types of interviews.

Multiple Interviewers

- Make eye contact with each person in the room at some point during the interview and direct your answers to everyone. Do not concentrate all your attention on the person who seems the nicest or is giving you the most reassuring look.

- Speak up. You will probably be in a larger room and your voice may not carry. You may feel like you are shouting, but it's important to project what you are saying to every corner of the room.

Group Interviews

- You don't want to interrupt or dominate the conversation, but you don't want to be left out, either. At least a few times, try to be the first one to answer.

- If you answer second or third, remind yourself that it allows you time to think.

- Remember, you are as deserving as the other candidates, and the interviewers want to hear what you have to say.

One-on-One Interviews

- Take advantage of this opportunity to really connect with the interviewer and to spend a few minutes discussing something you have in common. Show there's a lot more to you than being a quiet person.

- Don't get carried away, though; leave time for the interview questions.

- Draw on your background research to ask a question that shows you are prepared and interested. Even if the question has been answered earlier, the interviewer can expand further.

Follow Up after the Interview

After your interview, write thank-you notes on business-appropriate stationery or cards (no funny cartoons or distracting designs) to every person with whom you spoke. If you can, summarize a few points from your discussions or refer to an insight the person shared with you. Reiterate your interest in the position, tell them how much you enjoyed speaking with them, and express appreciation for their time.

Write and send your notes promptly, within a few days of your interview.

Conclusion

No matter what your personality type—shy or outgoing, bold or reserved—you can excel during the interview by planning in advance, doing research to become familiar with each program, and practicing your responses to common interview questions. Project confidence, and always remember to smile.

Chapter 8

The Match

By Deanna Kania and Monica L. Miller

We call it "the Match," but what we're talking about is the Residency Matching Program, a program sponsored and supervised by the American Society of Health-System Pharmacists (ASHP). Run by the National Matching Services (NMS), the same group that places physicians into residencies, the Match links residency candidates with accredited postgraduate year 1 (PGY1) and postgraduate year 2 (PGY2) residencies (and those seeking accreditation) using an algorithm that takes preferences and other data into account.

After you have submitted applications to residency programs and completed the interview process, it's time to narrow your choice of programs down to the ones you truly want—and to participate in the Match. You can begin registering for the Match in October, but you should definitely register by the following January, because you can't submit residency applications through the Pharmacy Online Residency Centralized Application Service (PhORCAS) until you're registered for the Match.

Before you register for the Match and apply to programs, you have a lot to do. This chapter

Turn in your rank order list early. If you wait until the last hour, the computer system will be bogged down with thousands of people turning in their results. You don't want to run the risk of missing the deadline due to a slow system. If you miss the deadline, you don't get a residency.

—Isabel Hagedorn

discusses selecting the programs you want to apply for, the matching process, the post-match "Scramble," and what to do if your "Plan A" does not come through. See Table 8-1 for a listing of key dates related to the Match.

Table 8-1 | **Match Timeline**

Month	Activity
August	Residency program directors (RPDs) complete Residency Agreements for participation in the Match.
October	Registration opens for applicants.
November	Program listings are available.
Early January	Time period when all applicants should be registered for the Match.
Early February	Instructions are sent to applicants and RPDs on how to submit respective rank order lists.
	Applicants and programs can begin submitting rank order lists and can change them up until the final rank order list submission date.
Early March	Final date that an applicant can register for the Match.
	Final date for rank order list submission by both applicants and programs—usually the day after the final Match registration date. No rank order lists can be submitted or changes made to lists after this date.
Match Day	About two weeks after your final rank list is due.
One month from Match Day	Applicants must receive from RPDs and sign a letter of confirmation of the Match results; they then must return the letter to the RPD.

Narrowing Your Residency List

If you have been lucky enough to interview with several residency programs, you will now need to decide which are the most desirable for you. Where would you like to spend the next year? You must compare the different programs, as you did when you decided where to send applications in Chapter 6. Review the list you created about things that are important to you and compare it with information you collected from each of the programs with which you interviewed. Think about all the positive aspects as well as drawbacks to each program. Besides looking at the facts, listen to your gut. Often, intangible things can make you like one program better than the rest. Can you truly see yourself working at this site every day and becoming a part of the pharmacy team?

After whittling your list to the programs that interest you the most, rank them from your highest to your lowest preference. There is no limit to the number of programs you can rank, but be aware that the shorter the list, the greater the chance for remaining unmatched from a program. On the opposite side, don't include a program that you really didn't like just for the sake of trying to match, because you might end up with that program—and ultimately you may be dissatisfied. The best way to achieve a good match is to rank only the programs in which you have a true interest. Once your "rank order list" is complete, you can submit it to the NMS.

"My approach for selecting my top program involved lots of contemplation," said Isabel Hagedorn, who applied to four PGY1 residencies in 2009. After completing her interviews, she asked herself several questions, including, "Can I see myself staying here for a second-year residency, if that's the path I decide to pursue? Do I fit in with the program, coworkers, other residents, and preceptors? Or did I feel uncomfortable and out of the loop during my interview? How will the residency affect my life goals and ambitions?"

Hagedorn recommends that you avoid ranking any program with which you wouldn't be happy to be matched. "One of my friends cried when she found out where she matched, because she didn't want to go there," Hagedorn said. "Don't let that happen to you. If at any point in the process you can't see yourself content and thriving in a program, drop it."

The questions in Sidebar 8-1 can help you rank the residency programs you have selected for matching.

On the day the Match results came out and I found I did not match with a PGY1 residency, I began the Scramble process. I reviewed the list of unmatched programs, looked at websites for programs in my chosen geographic area, and sent a cover letter and CV to the appropriate people. Most had filled their unmatched positions, and my rejections piled up. I sent emails to programs in areas of the country I hadn't originally thought about moving to. Two allowed me to apply by sending reference letters and transcripts. I interviewed with one by telephone, and they offered me the position the next day. It was very hard to decide to move to Indiana from Connecticut, but I did it, and I have no regrets.

— Colleen Teevan

Sidebar 8-1. Ranking Considerations for the Match

How you rank the programs that interest you is a personal choice. This list of questions can guide you, but ultimately, you must decide which factors matter most to you.

- What does each program provide that is important to me?

- What are the differences between the programs?

- How many resident positions does each program have?

- What are the research, teaching, and/or precepting requirements?

- What career paths have previous residents taken?

- What opportunities are available to collaborate with other institutions?

- What is the staffing component?

- Does the site have a PGY2 residency in a specialty that interests me?

- Could I live in the city in which the program is located?

- Do I feel like I could get along with the preceptors and residency directors?

- Do I agree with the program's values and objectives?

- Is the program a good fit for me and my personality?

- Will the program allow me to meet my professional goals?

How the Match Works

The Match links the applicant's highest preference with the program's highest preference. To match with a program in the first round, the order in which you rank the program must match the order in which that same program ranks you.

Let's say that you rank three programs (A, B, and C), and each of these programs has three residency positions. If "A" is your first choice, the "A" program would have to rank you 1, 2, or 3 to create a match (remember, each program in the example has three positions).

If you rank program "A" as your first choice and it has only one residency position, and program "A" ranks you as number two, you will not match on the first round. However, you could still match with program "A" if its number one candidate gets matched with a different program. You would move up from number two to number one and make a match. This all happens behind the scenes of the NMS; applicants and programs are never notified how a party ranked them. Both applicants and programs learn the final results on Match day. Some key rules of the Match appear below.

> The best way to achieve a good match is to rank only the programs in which you have a true interest.

- Results of the Match constitute a binding agreement between the participant and the residency site. Neither the applicant nor the program can withdraw without mutual written agreement from both parties. Each program must offer an appointment to each applicant with whom it is matched, and the applicant must accept the offer from the program unless both parties agree in writing to release each other from the binding Match result.

- Match participants are not allowed to solicit ranking-related information. Programs may not state their ranking intentions to applicants, and they cannot inquire about how they rank on an applicant's list. Similarly, applicants cannot ask programs about ranking intentions.

- You can rank as many or as few residency programs as you would like; there is no maximum or minimum number.

- You can update your rank order list as often as you like between the first date available to enter your top preferences (typically in February) and the registration close day in March.

Key Steps and Tips

Before you can be matched, you must register for the Match online using the registration portal shared by the Match and PhORCAS. (Find the portal at https://portal.phorcas.org or www.natmatch.com/ashprmp.) To register, you pay a nonrefundable fee by check or credit card; in 2013, the fee was $116.

Next you create your rank order list by entering your top preferences of programs using the web-based Rank Order List Input and Confirmation system, which opens for use in early February. Important tips for creating your rank order list include the following:

- Rank more than one program.

- Select programs that are right for you.

- Rank only the programs in which you want to participate.

- Do not try to guess how a program will rank you.

- Do not include a program based on a fear that you will not be matched anywhere else.

- Do not feel bad about not ranking a program. You are not obligated to include a program just because they interviewed you.

- Double check your list before hitting the submit button.

Applying with a Partner

If you have a spouse or significant other who is going through the residency application process at the same time, you can enroll in the Match as a couple. This allows you to coordinate your residency selections more easily, but you have to work together to decide on your rank list. For more information about the specifics of this program, please see the ASHP Residency Matching Program website at www.natmatch.com/ashprmp/applcouple.html or search the site for "how to participate as a couple."

Match Day

Match Day is the day that programs and residents find out who has been matched with particular programs. The NMS will email you by around noon Eastern Standard Time on Match Day to let you know your results—so be sure you have supplied an accurate email address. It's an exciting day for both programs and soon-to-be residents, but it can also be a sad day if you do not get matched. Be prepared for either result.

"I remember refreshing my email inbox every five seconds waiting for the results," says Joshua Raub, who completed a PGY1 residency with Johns Hopkins in 2010. "Once the email arrived, I immediately scrolled down to the results and probably had to read the match result half a dozen times before it finally registered in my brain." Ashley Johns, who completed her residency at the University of California at Irvine Medical Center in 2006, recalls that she "felt relief that I matched but sadness I didn't get my top choice. However, I am happy how it turned out."

Colleen Teevan was on rotation on Match Day and couldn't get on the Internet until she finally got a chance to stop by the computers in the hospital library. "I found out that I did not match, and I was devastated," she said. "Somehow I made it through the rest of the rotation day and when I got home, I cried."

Do not let negative results discourage you. Everything happens for a reason, and just because you don't match doesn't mean you can't end up with a wonderful residency as a result of the Scramble. And even if that option does not work out, you will find the perfect job or experience for you—just keep your options open.

—Ashley Crumby

The results of the matching process are something that should be shared, but how you share that information is a personal choice. We think you should answer honestly to people who inquire about the results you received, but avoid boasting to friends after the results are posted. Some people you know will not match to a residency program and will feel upset. Be respectful and supportive of their situation.

If you are not matched with a residency program on Match Day, it's okay. You have another option—"the Scramble." Colleen Teevan, for example, worked through the Scramble list over the next few days and ended up doing a residency at St. Joseph Regional Medical Center in Mishawaka, Indiana.

The Scramble

Approximately 40% of residency applicants do not match, so if it happens to you, you're not alone. Take a deep breath and decide whether to go through the post-match process, commonly called the Scramble. In the Scramble, students and programs that did not match try to find each other. The process can be stressful and emotional, but it's important to keep your goals in perspective and to behave professionally as you proceed.

PhORCAS will post a list on its website of all the residencies still available. This list is continually updated to show which positions have been filled. Your school or college of pharmacy can be a great help if you are participating in the Scramble. Some have faculty available to help students quickly review application materials after the Match. Before Match Day, find out if such assistance is available at your school, so you know how to benefit from it if you need to. Sidebar 8-2 contains guidance for managing the Scramble.

At press time, ASHP was considering developing a more formal post-match process that would possibly include a second electronic match. A date would be set for candidates and programs to submit a second rank list, and then another match would be initiated. To learn of any changes or new post-match processes, check the ASHP website at www.ashp.org.

Your "Plan B"

What happens if the post-match Scramble does not secure you a residency position? No doubt you will feel very disappointed. Please do not view the lack of a match as a reflection on your skills or potential. The Match and the Scramble are complicated, highly competitive processes, and even being selected for residency interviews is an indication of your value. Although a residency is an excellent way to gain postgraduate training to jump-start your career, it is *not the only way*. If you end up without a match, count it as a blessing in disguise and re-evaluate how you want to launch your pharmacy career. Ask yourself these questions:

- What are my five-year professional goals and can I achieve them without a residency?

Sidebar 8-2. Steps for Managing the Post-Match Scramble

- Review the list of programs with open residency positions listed on the PhORCAS site.

- Identify and learn more about programs that may interest you. You can review program websites or contact the RPD for additional information about the program.

- Gather program contact information from PhORCAS for each of your desired programs and send it to the people writing your letters of recommendation.

- Contact the programs via email or phone as soon as you are organized and ready—with your application fully compiled. If the program requires any additional forms, as indicated through PhORCAS, prepare and submit them.

- Work with faculty and staff at your school or college of pharmacy to get any assistance they can offer, such as helping you fill out applications or putting you in touch with people they know at residencies with openings that interest you.

- Programs will have access to all your previous materials on PhORCAS, including letters of recommendation. On rare occasions, you may encounter a program that has chosen not to enroll in PhORCAS, in which case you must send all required application materials to the program directly. Be prepared for another interview—which might be conducted on site, over the telephone, or using an online video chat service such as Skype.

- Where do I want to be 10 years from now, both professionally and personally? For my professional goal, do I need a residency to accomplish it?

- What postgraduate programs does my college of pharmacy offer?

- Is there a site that offers a nontraditional residency program that has a pharmacist position currently available? If so, then maybe I could complete a residency at that site.

- Would I be willing to reapply for a residency position next year?

Based on your answers to these questions, you may consider reapplying for a residency the next year.

When applying for residencies, have a "plan B"—as well as a plan C and D. Opportunities will always be available to reapply for a residency position in the future. Before you reapply, stay active in pharmacy organizations; continue to do community service; provide presentations; precept students; submit a poster to a local; state; or national meeting; continue to stay in touch with potential programs; attend regional residency showcases; and go to the ASHP Midyear Clinical Meeting before your target year to optimize your chances of obtaining a residency program the second time around.

Conclusion

The Match process can be stressful. Compare and contrast programs before submitting your choices, and rank only the programs where you would really be willing to spend an entire year. Do not rank programs you are lukewarm about or don't like.

Ensure that you have a Plan B in case the Match and Scramble processes do not yield a residency site for you. Obtaining a residency position is competitive. Be prepared for alternatives just in case. No matter what the outcome of the Match is, you are still a strong candidate for whatever path you choose to follow in pharmacy.

Chapter 9

Pharmaceutical Industry Fellowships

By Myra Wooley, Mina Alsaraf,
Joseph A. Barone, and Monica L. Miller

Another postgraduate training opportunity you may want to consider is a pharmaceutical industry fellowship. Industry fellowships can allow you to explore unique roles for pharmacists within the pharmaceutical industry and also help you launch a career in an area that interests you.

In recent years, industry fellowships have expanded into sectors that include clinical development, risk management, regulatory affairs, marketing, and health outcomes research, among many others. Sidebar 9-1 outlines some of the many areas in which fellowships are available. Later in this chapter, we will discuss each of these areas in more detail.

Fellowships are offered by a number of academic institutions and pharmaceutical companies, most of which are based on the East Coast. This chapter contains information about these types of programs and also discusses how to be well prepared if you choose to pursue a pharmaceutical industry fellowship.

> Industry fellowships can allow you to explore unique roles for pharmacists within the pharmaceutical industry and also help you launch a career in an area that interests you.

Sidebar 9-1. Pharmaceutical Industry Divisions and Types of Fellowships Offered

Here are some of the most common types of pharmacy fellowships:

Medical Affairs
- Medical Information/Communications

- Medical Strategy

- Field Medical/Medical Science Liaison

- Continuing Medical Education

- Health Economics and Outcomes Research

Commercial
- Marketing (consumer, professional, and payer)

- Business Development/Pharmaceutical Partnering/Mergers and Acquisitions

- Market Research/Analytics

- Business Intelligence

- Field Sales (sales representatives) and Sales Training

Market Access/Managed Markets
- Policy and Advocacy

- Health Economics and Outcomes Research

- Market Strategy

Clinical Research and Development
- Clinical Development (Preclinical/Phase I-II studies)

- Clinical Development (Phase II-IV studies)

- Clinical Trial Operations

- Risk Management

Regulatory Affairs
- U.S. Regulatory Affairs

- Global Regulatory Affairs

- Advertising/Promotions

Fellowship Focus Areas

Some of the most common categories for pharmacy fellowships include Medical Affairs, Commercial, Market Access/Managed Markets, Clinical Research and Development, and Regulatory Affairs. Across the pharmaceutical industry, effective work operations often involve the input of multiple individuals; you may hear this referred to as "matrix teams" or "working cross-functionally." Your fellowship will likely involve working collaboratively with different teams within your specialty area, such as Legal, Compliance, Clinical Research and Operations, Pricing, Marketing, Field Sales, Manufacturing, Public Relations, and Government Affairs.

Medical Affairs

The largest concentration of fellowships is found in medical divisions of pharmaceutical companies. Medical Affairs fellowships fall into several categories. Medical Information/Communications positions may involve responding to questions from patients and providers and making sure that drug promotional materials are based on clinical and scientific data and are compliant with requirements from the Food and Drug Administration (FDA) and regulatory agencies in other countries. The Medical Strategy/Scientific Affairs area determines unmet medical needs and develops key opinion leader (KOL) interactions. KOLs are scientific or medical experts in specific disease states who can be instrumental in helping the industry address unmet medical needs through research and education.

In the Field Medical/Medical Science Liaison area, fellows may dialogue with KOLs, medical professionals, and academics about products and provide nonsales and scientific field support. Continuing Medical Education, also known as Independent Medical Education, may involve deciding whether independent medical education about a product is necessary for patients or health care providers and following up after the education is provided to assess its effectiveness and outcomes. Fellows in Health Economics and Outcomes Research (HEOR) or Health Services conduct cost-effectiveness research for products and analyze data based on the needs of payers. This research can support payer decisions for both small and large institutions and health insurance providers. See Sidebar 9-2 for a summary of fellows' roles in Medical Affairs.

Sidebar 9-2. Summary of Fellows' Roles in Medical Affairs

- Answer patient and provider questions and urgent inquiries.

- Assess medical accuracy of promotional materials.

- Develop KOL plans.

- Determine unmet medical needs.

- Dialogue with KOLs on products.

- Provide nonsales scientific field support.

- Create and lead continuing education programs.

- Assess independent medical education effectiveness and outcomes.

- Conduct cost-effectiveness research studies.

- Evaluate HEOR data needs of payers.

- Support investigator-initiated studies by nonaffiliated health care providers.

Commercial

Your fellowship in this area might involve learning about different aspects of the commercialization process for a pharmaceutical agent. In addition, fellows in the commercial area strengthen their business acumen and enhance their clinical understanding of disease states.

Within the Commercial bucket of fellowships, Marketing involves promoting products to different populations: patients (consumers), professionals (health care providers), and payers (insurance companies or government purchasers). The Business Development/Pharmaceutical Partnering/ Mergers and Acquisitions area may include the merger and/or acquisition of new molecular entities from smaller or other large biopharmaceutical companies that discovered them. Market Research/Analytics is an area that provides information and assesses marketplace dynamics for use in the branding of pharmaceutical products. Business Intelligence provides information about the competitive landscape for a product.

Finally, the Sales organization trains representatives and sends them into the "field," or to various regions around the country, to educate customers about their product. Depending on the focus of the fellowship, fellows may be involved in training sales representatives. See Sidebar 9-3 for a summary of fellows' roles in the Commercial area.

Sidebar 9-3. Summary of Fellows' Roles in Commercial Area

- Be involved in the merger/acquisition of new molecular entities.

- Develop brand strategy and value proposition.

- Prepare key messages for sales teams.

- Execute marketing strategies to drive commercial performance.

- Conduct qualitative and quantitative market research.

- Provide analytical support to aid in business decision-making process.

- Identify, collect, analyze, and gather information about competitive landscape of brand.

Market Access/Managed Markets

Fellowship opportunities in market access, also called managed markets, can be found in the commercial, medical, or corporate affairs divisions, depending on the position. Students interested in these fellowships should look at resources such as the International Society of Pharmacoeconomics and Outcomes and the Academy of Managed Care Pharmacy. These groups provide online learning centers, publications, database digests, and tools to support health economics and outcomes research. Having prior knowledge of payers, perhaps through an internship, clerkship, or insurance company position, may be helpful when applying for a fellowship in Market Access.

Market Access/Managed Markets encompasses three areas. The first, Policy and Advocacy, focuses on important changes in regulations affecting public payers (commonly Medicare and Medicaid) and the external patient and professional advocacy community. A fellowship in this area will help you understand state and federal policies and determine their impact on the patient and professional community.

The second area, Health Economics and Outcomes Research, assesses the cost-effectiveness and real-world impact of a drug. Researchers in this area also provide data to supplement clinical efficacy and safety information for a product—information that a payer may request to aid in formulary decision-making. Cost-effectiveness analyses are frequently measured in cost per health utility gained or prevented, such as time-to-relapse, length of hospitalization, or improvements in patient survival.

The final specialty area is Markets Strategy. Fellows in this area analyze data to help understand the priorities of payers and develop strategies for pricing and reimbursement, as well as communication messages to payers. See Sidebar 9-4 for a summary of fellows' roles in Market Access/Managed Markets.

Sidebar 9-4. Summary of Fellows' Roles in Market Access/ Managed Markets

- Liaise with external advocacy organizations to advance patient care.

- Research legislative and market access policies to develop internal policy positions.

- Conduct cost-effectiveness research for products.

- Evaluate HEOR data needs of payers.

- Understand payer priorities and how they impact products and patient access.

- Develop pricing and reimbursement strategy.

Clinical Research

Clinical research is the sector of the pharmaceutical industry that determines how to develop a pharmaceutical compound, conduct research to demonstrate safety and efficacy, and prepare for filing with the FDA or another regulatory body. Clinical research fellowships may include preclinical/translational medicine research, Phase I first in human trials, and Phase II-IV clinical trials for safety and efficacy.

The Clinical Trial Operations area manages the logistics of clinical trials, from selecting vendors and communicating with contract organizations to overseeing quality managing research sites. The Risk Management area involves evaluating a product's safety profile throughout its development and preparing information to ensure safe use of the product. See Sidebar 9-5 for a summary of fellows' roles in Clinical Research.

Sidebar 9-5. Summary of Fellows' Roles in Clinical Research

- Develop protocols and informed consent.

- Study site-initiation and close-out visits.

- Monitor study data throughout trials.

- Conduct medical writing and support statistical/programming teams in creating study reports.

- Contribute to ongoing scientific review, analysis, reporting, and publishing of clinical data.

- Select and manage external service providers and clinical research organizations.

- Help develop clinical sections of regulatory documents.

- Ensure that studies are run in accordance with international and local regulations and good clinical practices.

Regulatory Affairs

A final area that produces many pharmacy fellowships is Regulatory Affairs. These fellowships usually fall into three broad categories: U.S. Regulatory Affairs, Global Regulatory Affairs, and Advertising/Promotions.

The U.S. and Global Regulatory Affairs departments submit to the FDA, or to international regulatory agencies, applications that are required for new drugs or new indication approvals. Advertising/Promotions staff oversee the approval of promotional materials to meet the FDA Office of Prescription Drug Promotion standards and may also help develop the prescribing information that becomes the official label/package insert for a drug. Frequently, a team of representatives from the Legal, Medical, and

Regulatory departments review promotional materials to ensure compliance and accuracy of claims. See Sidebar 9-6 for a summary of fellows' roles in Regulatory Affairs.

Sidebar 9-6. Summary of Fellows' Roles in Regulatory Affairs

- Work to submit required applications (Investigational New Drug, New Drug Application, and Biologics License Applications) to the FDA (U.S. Regulatory Affairs) or corresponding global regulatory bodies (Global Regulatory Affairs).

- Observe label negotiations between the FDA and the manufacturer.

- Submit required applications to global regulatory bodies.

- Monitor compliance with regulations on promotional claims ensuring "fair balance" of safety and efficacy.

- Participate in legal, medical, and regulatory review of promotional materials prior to entering the field for sales/medical education.

Fellowship Positions

Now that you're aware of some of the areas in which you might find a fellowship, you will want to consider who offers these programs and where they are located. Some fellowships are affiliated with pharmacy schools and others with individual pharmaceutical companies or pharmaceutical consultants. Tables 9-1 and 9-2 list some available academic and industry fellowships as of 2012. You can find the most up-to-date information by checking with your pharmacy school or the individual drug companies that interest you.

As the pharmaceutical industry evolves to meet the demands of the marketplace, fellowship offerings will change. As of 2012, the number of HEOR, Regulatory Affairs, Business Development, and Medical Affairs fellowships were on the rise. You will want to check for current trends when you apply for fellowships to give yourself the best information about your prospects for future employment. Table 9-3 lists some sources of news on the pharmaceutical industry.

Table 9-1 | **University Affiliated Fellowship Offerings as of 2012**

School Affiliation	Company	State
Florida A & M	Bristol-Myers Squibb	New Jersey
Massachusetts College of Pharmacy & Health Sciences	Biogen Idec Cubist Pharmaceuticals	Massachusetts
	Genzyme Biopharmaceutical	Massachusetts
	Novartis	Massachusetts
	Pfizer Inc.	Massachusetts
Philadelphia College of Pharmacy University of the Sciences	Johnson & Johnson Consumer	New Jersey
	Med Val & Pharma Write	New Jersey, Pennsylvania
Purdue University	Eli Lilly + FDA[&]	Indiana and Maryland
Rutgers University	Bristol-Myers Squibb	New Jersey
	Acorda Therapeutics	New Jersey
	Janssen	New Jersey
	Bayer Health Care	New Jersey
	TKL Research	New Jersey
	Merck	New Jersey
	Daiichi-Sankyo	New Jersey
	Johnson & Johnson	New Jersey
	Sunovion	New Jersey
	Novartis	New Jersey
	Roche	New Jersey
	Pfizer Consumer	New Jersey
St. John's University	Forest Pharmaceuticals*	New Jersey, New York
	Daiichi Sankyo*	New Jersey, New York
	American Regeant*	New York

continued on page 150

149

Table 9-1 | **University Affiliated Fellowship Offerings as of 2012,**
continued

Thomas Jefferson University	Janssen*	New Jersey, Pennsylvania
	Novartis	New Jersey, Pennsylvania
University of Arizona	Allergan	Arizona
University at Buffalo	Novartis	New Jersey, New York
University of California, San Francisco	Biogen Idec	California, Massachusetts
University of Illinois at Chicago		Illinois
University of Maryland	Novartis	Maryland, New Jersey
University of the Sciences in Philadelphia (USP)⁺	Genentech	Greater Philadelphia and San Francisco, California
University of Southern California*	Allergen	California
	ISTA	California
University of Texas	Novartis with Scott & White Health Plan*	Texas, New Jersey
University of Utah	Novartis	Utah
University of Washington	Allergan	Washington, California
West Virginia University School of Pharmacy	ISTA	West Virginia

⁺This program is offered only to USP graduates.
& This program is a dual program that offers a fellowship at Eli Lilly and the FDA.
* Fellowships offer degree granting.

Source: Adapted from CareerPharm. ASHP's Career Community. Available at:
http://www.careerpharm.com/careertools.aspx.

Table 9-2 | **Industry-Sponsored and Consultant Fellowships**

Fellowship Sponsor	Company	Location
Industry Company Fellowships	Abbott PharmD Development Program	Illinois
	Eli Lilly Visiting Scientist Program	Indiana
	Johnson & Johnson	New Jersey
	Novo Nordisk	New Jersey
	Upsher-Smith Laboratories	Minnesota
	Genentech – Commercial Rotation Development Program	California
Pharmaceutical Industry Consultants	MED Communications, Inc.	Tennessee
	Xcenda*	Florida

Fellowships offer degree granting

Heightened Payer Involvement

Payers have become increasingly important in the health care system and in drug development—which means that pharmaceutical companies have to consider their needs as early as the Phase II phase of clinical development, possibly leading to an increase in employment opportunities in HEOR, Policy and Advocacy, and Managed Markets.

Medical Device and Dual Drug-Device Agents

Opportunities for pharmacists are also growing in areas that involve medical device manufacturing. The increasing development of novel drug delivery systems such as inhalers and implants that include drug-elusion can open doors for PharmD graduates to work closely with engineers and formulation experts, and to be involved in medical and commercial education to patients, prescribers, and payers.

Development of Biotechnology Products

Innovation in the areas of orphan drugs, oncology, and large molecules is expanding. A fundamental understanding of immunotherapy and immunology will be helpful if you are seeking a fellowship in these areas, as will undergraduate or graduate research experience.

Table 9-3 | Helpful News Feeds on the Pharmaceutical Industry

Site Name	Description	Website	Cost
Fierce Pharma	Provides trending news in the pharmaceutical and biopharmaceutical industry, as well as some health care information.	www.fiercepharma.com	Free
Fierce Healthcare	Provides trending news in health care, generally from the provider or health system point of view.	www.fiercehealthcare.com	Free
FirstWord	Provides business intelligence for pharmaceutical and biopharmaceutical companies.	www.firstwordplus.com	Free
Pink Sheet	A business development and commercialization resource with in-depth coverage of regulatory, legal, financial, and executive changes.	www.elsevierbi.com/publications/the-pink-sheet	Expensive; your university may or may not have access
Medscape	Provides literature updates for various medical conditions and practitioners. Subscribe to "Medscape Pharmacists" daily news feeds to keep abreast of Food and Drug Administration label changes and clinical updates.	www.medscape.com	Free
ASHP Daily Briefing	Daily summary of relevant clinical updates in health care.	www.ashp.org/s_ashp/doc1c.asp?CID=167&DID=7813	Available to ASHP members only

Information and Digital Technology

There is a growing need for individuals who can converse in the "digital language" of health care. Whether you have an interest in clinical trial operations, medical information, or the commercial side of the pharmaceutical industry, your information technology experience can be an asset as you apply for fellowships. Experience using various social media platforms and operating digital software, such as iPad applications and QR codes, can also help you be more competitive.

Compensation and Certification

As a pharmacy fellow, you will receive a stipend and benefit package, including comprehensive health insurance. Compensation varies, but as of 2012 competitive salaries ranged from $40,000 to $50,000 per year. Benefits may be provided through the partnering university or pharmaceutical company. Often, your paid attendance at professional meetings, conferences, or workshops will be included as part of your compensation package.

Most fellowships award a certificate upon successful completion of the program. Some universities, including the University of Washington, Thomas Jefferson University, and St. John's, offer the opportunity to work toward a postgraduate degree during your fellowship period. If obtaining a postgraduate degree is important to you, be sure it's a feasible option during your fellowship.

A Timeline for Your Fellowship

While most of the activities involved in your fellowship search will be concentrated in your final year of pharmacy school, you will be exploring opportunities throughout your years of schooling. You can find a breakdown of the items involved in your fellowship search in Figure 9-1 and Sidebar 9-7.

Some fellowships are affiliated with pharmacy schools and others with individual pharmaceutical companies or consultants.

Figure 9-1 | Timeline for Pharmaceutical Industry Fellowships

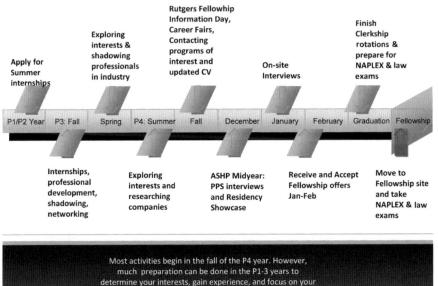

Most activities begin in the fall of the P4 year. However, much preparation can be done in the P1-3 years to determine your interests, gain experience, and focus on your professional growth

Sidebar 9-7. Timing of Steps for an Industry Fellowship

P1/P2 Year:

- Focus on exploring opportunities and taking advantage of summer internships offered by companies and government agencies. A listing of internships can be found at: http://pharmafellows.rutgers.edu/about/index.php

- Applications for these programs are due between February and April each year.

- During your P2 year, pursue summer internships and endeavor to have clerkship rotations in industry settings or the FDA.

P3 Year:

- Identify your interests.

- Spend time on your professional development and seek out opportunities to shadow and network with professionals in industry.

- Continuously update your curriculum vitae (CV).

- Build a network of contacts including current fellows, professionals in industry, and professors.

Sidebar 9-7, *continued*

- Attend career fairs to speak with fellowship representatives and attend lectures pertaining to developments in the pharmaceutical industry.

- Subscribe to and review a service that provides updates on industry happenings.

P4 Year Summer:
- Spend time narrowing your area of interest.

- Spell out your curiosities and career goals and match these to a few of the fellowship focus areas.

- Research websites of the schools and companies offering fellowship positions in your focus areas.

- Ask questions of alumni of your school who have completed the fellowship in which you are interested.

P4 Year Fall:
- Attend regional pharmacy school career fairs and residency showcases to network and refine your interests.

- Attend the Rutgers Fellowship Information and Networking Day.

- Contact current fellows and preceptors to show your interest in their program.

- Register for the Personnel Placement Service (PPS) in preparation for scheduling interviews at the Midyear Clinical Meeting (MCM).

- Update your CV for the PPS and MCM.

P4 Year December:
- Attend the MCM of the American Society of Health-System Pharmacists (ASHP).

- Participate in the fellowship showcase and schedule interviews.

- Attend company receptions.

P4 Year January/February:
- Submit applications (many require supplemental application materials).

- Participate in on-site interviews.

- Accept a fellowship offer. (Fellowships do not utilize the Match program, as residencies do.) Offers are made at varying times throughout January and February; expect a short turnaround time for accepting or declining.

Networking

As you finish your schooling and become more involved in your pharmacy career, your professional network will continue to be a valuable resource. You may be surprised how small the pharmacy world can seem, and the pharmaceutical industry is no different. You might cross paths with former schoolmates, co-fellows, and coworkers at any time as you, and they, change jobs and companies.

During your fellowship search, and after, you may want to participate in alumni events, seminars, professional meetings, and career fairs to establish and sustain relationships. Social media such as the LinkedIn professional network can serve as an online business card, which allows you to keep your profile updated and build your contact list. Make opportunities to connect with colleagues—you can do something as simple as sharing an article via email that might be of interest to them.

Also, consider participating in the various networking and support groups sponsored by your organization. These may be targeted toward women, members of ethnic minorities, or people who share particular professional interests.

Rutgers Fellowship Information and Networking Day

The Fellowship Information and Networking Day, previously called the Fellowship Information Day, is a one-day event sponsored by the Rutgers Institute for Pharmaceutical Industry Fellowships. It is typically held in Piscataway, New Jersey, in November and includes a program overview and networking.

ASHP Midyear Clinical Meeting

ASHP's MCM provides an excellent opportunity for you to interview with fellowship programs in which you are interested. Many companies will use Midyear encounters to determine which candidates they will invite to their on-site interviews.

If you can, schedule interviews with fellowship programs you're interested in before Midyear. You can utilize the PPS system to upload your CV and contact programs to set up interviews. (See Chapter 5 for information about this service.)

Interviews are conducted during the business portion of the day, but it's important to attend evening receptions and events, too, to network with program representatives. As in any interview situation, consider any event part of the process and be sure to conduct yourself professionally. Prepare for your interviews using the strategies discussed in Chapter 7. Sidebar 9-8 includes tips related to the MCM.

Application Process

The application process for industry fellowships is similar to that for residency programs. Each fellowship program may request a candidate to submit a CV, letter of intent, and two to three letters of recommendation. Among your references, it can help to have at least one from an industry mentor who can speak highly about your professionalism and leadership abilities.

Application deadlines range from December to January, but it is best to submit application materials as soon as you can so the program can begin scheduling on-site interviews.

The On-site Interview and Offer Acceptance

On-site fellowship interviews generally take place in late December or early January, during a workday. The company sponsoring the fellowship will often cover your expenses for travel, lodging, and meals.

During these interviews, you will meet with a variety of team members including program directors, preceptors, and current fellows. These program representatives will be deciding whether you are a good fit for their team, and you will be considering whether you would enjoy the work and if it will further your career goals.

Because fellowship programs do not participate in any kind of national matching service, a program can offer you a job opportunity very soon after your on-site interview. You'll have a brief period of time, ranging from two days to four weeks, after the offer is made to decide whether to accept. Sidebar 9-9 lists some factors to consider when you are making your decision. If you are applying for multiple fellowships within one program or different programs, let them know your specific situation so that appropriate time is given to your decision.

Sidebar 9-8. Preparing to Meet with Fellowship Programs at the ASHP Midyear Clinical Meeting

General

- Research careers in industry.
- Network with past fellows and pharmacy professionals in industry.
- Research companies so you can answer the question, "Why are you interested in our company?" Areas to investigate may include the following:
  - Therapeutic areas
  - Pipeline
  - Goals and mission statements
  - Philanthropy projects
  - Market plans
- Select programs that interest you.
- Polish and update your CV.
- Purchase business cards.
- Practice interviewing.
- Know your goals and what sets you apart.

MCM Receptions

- Attend MCM receptions if you are invited; these are by invitation only. Failing to attend is viewed negatively.
- Behave professionally.
- Introduce yourself to company personnel you have not yet met and leave a good impression by demonstrating that you know their company and department well.
- Interact with many people.

PPS Interviews

- Complete the Candidate Interest Form (the list of all fellowships conducting interviews).
- Register for first-round interviews before Midyear via PPS online or directly at the MCM. Additional interviews may be offered if you advance past the first interview.
- A standard set of questions is used for each interview candidate; interviews range from 15 to 45 minutes.
- Manage your time wisely. Because some interviews may run short or long, try not to schedule them back-to-back.
- Bring snacks, because you may not have time to eat between interviews.

Sidebar 9-9. Accepting Offers from Programs: Characteristics to Consider

Program Selection
- Strengths and weaknesses of program/company.

- Location.

- Learn how the program meets your professional goals.

- Compensation/benefits.

- Time frame (1 versus 2 years).

- Autonomy.

- Where past fellows are now.

Company Affiliations
- Retention rate.

- Fellowship opportunities.

- Company culture.

- Therapeutics areas.

- Supervisor.

- Prior experience with fellow.

- Support for professional development.

School Affiliations
- Preceptors.

- Opportunities to publish.

- Responsibilities.

- History of the program and school collaboration.

Job Placement Post-Fellowship

Working in a fellowship does not guarantee job placement. However, fellowship programs do help prepare you to find your next position by providing skills and connections that will help you in your search.

Post-fellowship, people may pursue careers with pharmaceutical companies, government agencies, the generics manufacturing industry, academia, consulting, managed care organizations, and professional association management. Or they may continue their education, pursuing a Master's in Business Administration, Master's in Public Health, Juris Doctor, or other graduate degree.

> The largest concentration of fellowships is found in medical divisions of pharmaceutical companies.

During your fellowship, you can look for opportunities to build your network and plan for your future. One of the best ways to do this is to immerse yourself in your company. Learn about the company's key business drivers, work with managers and mentors to develop goals, and provide appropriate input within your team and with coworkers. Being an involved employee benefits both you and the company; it also gives you a greater knowledge of the field of pharmacy.

You may also consider working with a recruiting agency to learn about employment options post-fellowship. Talk to your coworkers and professional contacts about their experiences to get recommendations for recruiters who have good reputations and achieve results within the pharmacy industry.

Advice from Former Fellows

The stories that follow from former industry fellows will help you learn more about different aspects of fellowship programs.

Jennifer Huntington
Clinical Research Fellow, Cubist Pharmaceuticals, Inc.;
now Senior Clinical Research Scientist at Cubist

As a fellow I was responsible for contributing scientific input to the clinical development activities of my group. Typical projects included researching and analyzing published literature and regulatory materials to develop quality clinical documents such as protocols, investigator's brochures, and briefing books. In addition, I worked closely with the medical monitor for each study to ensure successful execution of clinical trials. These independent activities were coupled with participation on multidisciplinary study and development teams to discuss progression and execution of clinical programs.

Although as a fellow my primary role was gaining experience and learning the intricacies of the clinical development program, I was often charged with leading discussions and overseeing projects related to the clinical programs on which I worked. I had an opportunity to function as an independent contributor, but I always had oversight and support.

The academic component of my fellowship offered many unique development opportunities that expanded upon my industry experience. I precepted students, developed and delivered lectures, and coordinated clinical courses with other faculty. The academic component emphasized mentorship and provided me with the opportunity to enhance my presentation and leadership skills.

The transition from being a fellow to an employee was fairly easy for me, because I was fortunate enough to be hired by the company where I completed my fellowship. The majority of my projects, as well as whom I reported to, remained the same, although the level of responsibility and independence increased. It was very rewarding to continue working on the same projects and have the ability to see them through to completion.

My fellowship training gave me the opportunity to observe many aspects of the pharmaceutical industry that I would not have been exposed to otherwise. The objective of a fellowship is to educate, develop, and mentor fellows, and there is broad support throughout the organization to provide fellows with ample opportunities to explore all areas of interest.

Consequently, I was able to shadow various groups outside of my home department including Medical Affairs, Regulatory Affairs, Commercial and Marketing, Clinical Operations, and Business Development. These opportunities allowed me to explore different career paths in a way that would not have been possible as a permanent employee.

Tiffany Marsh
Medical Strategy Fellow, Bristol-Myers Squibb;
now Regional Medical Liaison of Lantus Physician Training at Sanofi, Inc.

I chose to do a fellowship instead of residencies because I knew hospital pharmacy was not the way to go for me. If you are not certain about which path to take (clinical pharmacist versus industry pharmacist), a fellowship may not be as important for you. You could do a residency, become a clinical pharmacist, and work your way back to industry, but this will take more time and you will not have the level of networking that a fellowship gives you.

The broader impact that I could make brought me to industry. Sometimes in hospital and retail, the pharmacist has more of a one-on-one impact on patients, but I wanted to make an impact on a larger number of lives at the same time.

Go after as many opportunities as you possibly can during your fellowship because this is the time you are most likely to be given them—whether it is projects or interfacing with upper management. I tell my mentees/protégés to develop relationships with the other fellows. Your cofellows will be great allies for you later in life, and this is where professional friendships that can really be valuable moving forward are made.

I changed companies immediately after the fellowship, so I was forced to go outside my comfort zone and meet new individuals. I overcame this by using the communication and networking skills that I learned through my fellowship to gain visibility for my leadership at Sanofi. I met with them through one-on-ones and was bold enough to ask for assignments from them. One of the Senior Vice Presidents asked me to take minutes for a senior level meeting, which allowed me to gain visibility as well as provide a service to them. I learned this boldness through the fellowship program, by introducing myself, showing my value to the team, and securing an assignment from upper management within the 5-to-10 minute conversation that I had with the senior executive.

I think being a field medical professional is an excellent opportunity. It is an ever-evolving and exciting area within the industry, and I only see it getting better over time.

Joy Barclay
Non-Industry Fellowship;
now Executive Director of Global Commercialization for the HIV Franchise at Bristol-Myers Squibb

I did a fellowship in internal medicine because I knew I wanted to work in clinical practice and academia, and a clinical fellowship gives you more opportunity to do a research project. If you're interested in moving into industry immediately, an industry fellowship is a great way to get your foot in the door. It doesn't mean you cannot ever come into industry without an industry fellowship, as my example shows, but sometimes it is harder, especially as you are starting out.

One big mistake that individuals make starting new jobs or fellowships is that they are so eager to learn and absorb everything that they quickly get burned out. The best thing to do is to learn to prioritize your work. You're human; you can only do so much. Look to your manager and mentor to help set expectations up front. Be honest about your capacity and ask for help in prioritization. Remember, mentors and preceptors are there to help you. Don't view it as a weakness if you ask for help.

Having and being a mentor are very important. Having mentors is important because it becomes a trusting relationship where you can seek advice. I recommend having multiple mentors. These are people you can trust to give you honest, direct feedback. Being a mentor is also extremely important because it allows you to give back. Many people want to choose a similar path. Being a mentor allows me to help them because I have been there and have seen things so I can help facilitate the process for them.

Don't be afraid to do something because you're not sure of the outcome. I didn't do a fellowship in industry and didn't know much about it. After speaking to friends, I took a risk and figured, what do I have to lose?

I can go, interview, meet with others, and have a better understanding of what I like. I did that and found that the pharmaceutical industry really intrigued me—the whole aspect of taking my clinical background and my business side to a new level. You can marry the scientific/clinical side with the business and still deliver on the mission of helping people with serious diseases. I wouldn't change what I do in a million years because it helps me help the community and give back. It continues to make me energized and passionate.

Chapter 10

Before Starting Your Residency

By Monica L. Miller

Whoo HOO! You've made it through the anxiety of the residency application process and have secured your position! Now you have new things to consider as you transition to becoming a resident. This chapter talks about steps to take before starting your residency program and gives a few hints about getting off on the right foot.

Graduation

You have just worked very hard to obtain your residency position—and you're probably both excited and a bit overwhelmed at the prospect of everything you need to do in the weeks ahead. The first, most important thing is to *graduate from pharmacy school!* You can't start your residency program without that degree. As tempting as it may be, don't ease off during your upcoming rotations. Take advantage of the wonderful opportunity they give you to continue working on your drug knowledge and clinical skills. Then, when you finish your final rotation, celebrate! Graduation is just around the corner, and it's a major accomplishment you should be proud of.

> When you finish your final rotation, celebrate! Graduation is just around the corner, and it's a major accomplishment you should be proud of.

- Savor the last days together with your classmates.

- Take photos; you may think you'll remember every moment, but years later, you won't.

- Share your accomplishment with your family and friends.

- If your college of pharmacy has an end-of-year banquet, go to it.

- Attend graduation.

I can vividly remember the weekend of my graduation from the University of Minnesota College of Pharmacy. It was a great time, with lots of events taking place, all of them so exciting. My family came into Minneapolis and we went to my favorite restaurant for a celebratory dinner with a few close friends—all of whom had helped me through pharmacy school in one way or another. So that night, we were all celebrating what felt like a joint accomplishment. That dinner is still burned into my brain.

All of my 100 or so classmates were at the graduation ceremony, and I recall walking across the stage and hearing my name read as I was hooded. Wow, what a cool feeling. I remember thinking…I DID IT! No one can take this away. By the end of this fun weekend, I was starting to look forward to my move to Texas for my residency.

Licensure

Now the studying begins again. Before you can practice pharmacy, you have to become a licensed pharmacist—which means passing the NAPLEX (North American Pharmacist Licensure Examination) and MPJE (Multi-state Pharmacy Jurisprudence Examination). Most residencies require you to be licensed by August—roughly a month after you start the residency.

I advise you to take the NAPLEX and MPJE at least four or five days apart, if possible, which allows you time to study for the second exam and decompress a little from the first one. Do not take them on the same day, because you want to be in top form. They are high-stakes exams; you can't get licensed if you don't pass them. Although you can take the MPJE after you start your residency, it's best to get it out of the way beforehand so it's not hanging over your head. Sidebar 10-1 tells you how to register for these exams.

Sidebar 10-1. Registering for NAPLEX and MPJE

You must register for these exams before you can take them. Registration is allowed one to three weeks before graduation or when all of your experiential hours have been accounted for by the Office of Experiential Learning at your college or school of pharmacy. Do the following:

1. Review the application requirements for the state in which you want to be licensed.

2. Go to www.nabp.net and click on the link that says "CPE Monitor."

3. Create an electronic profile, if you haven't done so already.

4. Fill out all the appropriate information up to the point where the form asks for your license number. Once here, exit out of the web page.

5. Open a new web browser and go back to www.nabp.net. Click on the NAPLEX and MPJE application button to register for them both at once. (You don't take them on the same day, however. This registration simply puts you in line for your permission to take the tests.)

   • For your user name, input an email address you will be able to access after graduation.

   • Create a new user account.

   • Select the exam or score transfer you want to apply for.

   • In 2012, the NAPLEX cost was $485 and the cost of the score transfer, which is used when you apply for licensure in multiple states, was $75.

   • In 2012, the MPJE cost was $200.

NAPLEX

The NAPLEX tests your basic knowledge of pharmacy practice, and your pharmacy school has been preparing you to take it since your first day of classes. Don't panic. You know more than you think you do—but it is important to study. Many resources exist to help you prepare for the 185-question exam, so I won't go into detail here, but some key bullet points follow.

- Only 150 of the 185 questions are used to calculate your score; the other 35 are being tested for inclusion in future exams.

- The test uses an "adaptive" method, which means that when you answer a question, the computer program uses your right or wrong answer to select your upcoming questions from the question bank.

- You are allotted 4 hours and 15 minutes to take the exam.

- The NAPLEX questions are devised to test you on three broad areas:

  ○ Area 1: Assess Pharmacotherapy to Assure Safe and Effective Therapeutic Outcomes (56% of test).

  ○ Area 2: Assess Safe and Accurate Preparation and Dispensing of Medications (33% of test).

  ○ Area 3: Assess, Recommend and Provide Health Care Information That Promotes Public Health (11% of test).

- Test questions can be asked in a variety of formats:

  ○ Typical multiple choice (will likely have a case-based introduction that can be used for several multiple choice questions, or could be a solo question).

  ○ Multiple response, in which you select all answers that apply.

  ○ Math problems where the answer is written in by you.

  ○ Ordered response items, where you put things in the correct order.

  ○ Hot Spot items, which could be, for example, a diagram where you place mechanism of action information.

I clearly remember preparing for and taking the NAPLEX. Because I was really worried about passing, I attended review sessions and made sure to study, following the tips on the next page. On the day of the exam, I felt pretty stressed out beforehand, and when I finished the exam I felt happy, stupid, and exhausted. Then I started waiting for my score to come in the mail. The wait was painful, but the result was worth it. When I learned I had passed, I felt ecstatic!

Following are some quick study tips:

- Study for the exam for two to four weeks before you take it.

- Know your top 200 drugs.

    ○ This list is updated annually.

    ○ You can create or purchase flash cards.

    ○ Information to know: brand/generic names, metabolism, major drug interactions, therapeutics uses, available dosage forms, strengths, general class.

> Most residencies require you to be licensed by August—roughly a month after you start the residency.

- Attend a review session if possible (frequently offered by employers and pharmacy organizations, both national and local).

- Review therapeutic areas in which you are weak or uncomfortable.

- Review the competency statements provided to aid your studying.

- Practice calculations.

- Plan a study schedule.

- Invest in an up-to-date review book (examples below):

    ○ *The APhA Complete Review for Pharmacy*

    ○ *Kaplan NAPLEX Review*

    ○ *McGraw-Hill's NAPLEX Review Guide*

    ○ *PharmPrep: ASHP's NAPLEX Review*

    ○ *RxPrep's 2012 Course Book for NAPLEX Pharmacist Licensure Exam*

- Take a few practice exams and/or the Pre-NAPLEX .

Some important tips for taking the test effectively:

- Complete *all* questions.

- Answers *cannot* be changed once you submit your answer and move to the next question.

- Review the NAPLEX instructions module before beginning the exam.

- Read each question thoroughly.

- Do not leave the testing room without permission.

- Review all the rules before arriving at the testing center.

- Do not worry about the adaptive test questioning method. Answer each question to the best of your ability.

Your score is reported as a number, not a percentage. The minimum passing score is 75 and the maximum score is 150. The score is calculated based on the questions you answered correctly and the ability factor assigned to each question you answered. This scoring method means that, when you finish the exam, you won't be able to guess your score.

You can find your score online about seven days after you take the exam, if the state(s) you are becoming licensed in participate in the online score reporting system. (The online system is found at www.nabp.net/programs/examination/naplex/naplex-and-mpje-score-results). Otherwise, the score will be mailed to you, which may take longer than seven days.

MPJE
The MPJE, which tests your knowledge of state and federal law, is required by each state in which you plan to become licensed. It tests laws particular to the state as well as federal law. In my opinion, it's a harder exam than the NAPLEX, so be sure to study.

The two-hour exam has 90 questions; of these, 75 are scored and 15 are being assessed for future inclusion in the exam. Like the NAPLEX exam, the MPJE uses an adaptive questioning style. The minimum passing score is 75 and the maximum score is 100; as with the NAPLEX, these are not percentages but are scores based on the number correct and the difficulty level of the questions.

Some states and territories do not utilize the MPJE for their jurisprudence exams—specifically, Arkansas, California, Guam, Puerto Rico, Virginia, and the Virgin Islands. Contact the boards of pharmacy in these states to learn about testing requirements.

The MPJE is designed to test your knowledge in the following areas:

- Area 1: Pharmacy Practice (about 84% of the test).

- Area 2: Licensure, Registration, Certification, and Operational Requirements (about 13% of the test).

- Area 3: Regulatory Structure and Terms (about 3% of the test).

Test questions can be asked in several ways:

- Multiple choice

- Multiple answer

- Ordered format

The questions on this test can be hard and confusing. Many are situational, based on practice. Carefully read each scenario and question, as well as each possible answer. Some questions may seem as if there is no correct answer, while others appear to have multiple correct answers. Always select the *most* correct answer. Here is my list of essential study tips:

- Study for one or two weeks before the MPJE.

- Study both federal and state laws evenly.

- Attend a review session that covers both federal and state content.

- Answer practice questions found in reference books and materials.

- Purchase a good, up-to-date study guide:

○ *Guide to Federal Pharmacy Law* is a good resource for the federal portion.

○ For the state portion, ask current residents and residency directors in the state where you are getting licensed if they have recommendations of good study guides or class notes they can share. Many law professors have wonderful class notes that can be used to assist in learning the state laws.

I took three law exams because I am licensed in three states, and each one was tough for me. After finishing the tests, I walked out feeling like the least intelligent person on the planet and wondering, where did those questions come from? Many are geared to community practice. So I can't emphasize enough how important it is to study. And during the exam, read each question carefully.

When I was looking for study materials for the two exams outside of Minnesota, where I attended pharmacy school, I first checked each state's board of pharmacy website and called them. I also reached out to residency program members and faculty I knew in those states, and these methods yielded study materials that allowed me to prepare to the best of my ability.

Obtaining Testing Authorization

Testing authorization—that is, the "okay" for you to take the tests—is actually conveyed by the board of pharmacy in the states where you are applying for licensure. The board will review your licensure application materials, determine whether you are eligible to be licensed in that state, and then notify the National Association of Boards of Pharmacy (NABP) to give you testing authorization. If you have questions about your application or authorization, it is best to contact the state(s) to which you are applying for further information. Sidebar 10-2 spells out the steps in registering for licensure.

Applying for Licensure Outside Your State by Examination

If you will be doing a residency outside the state where you graduated from pharmacy school, notify your school's Office of Experiential Learning so the staff can help you obtain any documentation of experiential hours that may be required. Although the application process is similar in most states, there are exceptions.

Sidebar 10-2. License Registration Steps

To get a pharmacy license, submit an application to the state board of pharmacy. If your application is approved, you take the NAPLEX and MPJE. Once you pass (or fail) the tests, the NAPB notifies the board of pharmacy, which sends out your scores. You then send the state board a check for your annual license fee; there may be an additional fee for your first license.

Some states will mail you a license; others will have you print one from your computer. The process from step 12 below to having your license in hand can take up to a month or more, depending on the state and when you take the exams. You'll receive both a pocket license and one you can frame to hang in your office or workplace.

1. Obtain a passport photo (needed for your license application).

2. Receive the affidavit from your final rotation and a statement of the total number of experiential hours you will report to the board of pharmacy.

3. Submit your licensure application to the board of pharmacy of your choice.

4. Begin the background check process online at www.L1enrollment.com after your application is received by the board of pharmacy in the state you selected.

5. Verify that your pharmacy school or college has sent your Certification of Completion to the board of pharmacy after your graduation.

6. The board of pharmacy determines your eligibility to take the NAPLEX and MPJE and notifies the NABP.

7. The NABP issues an Authorization to Test (ATT) through Pearson VUE, which delivers exams through a secure network of test centers. The ATT, sent to you by email, includes the dates you are eligible to take the examination.

8. Register for NAPLEX/MPJE. You schedule your examination test dates and times at the Pearson's website (www.pearsonvue.com).

9. Take exams—preferably at least four to five days apart.

10. Receive your examination scores online about seven days after taking the exam, or by mail if the state you are becoming licensed in does not participate in the online score reporting system.

11. Pay for your pharmacy license.

12. Receive license by mail or online.

California, for example, requires completion of a California-specific affidavit for each of your rotation experiences. Illinois will reject your Certification of Education (the document stating that you have received your PharmD) if it is completed before you graduate. The lesson here is that you must contact the board of pharmacy in the state(s) where your residency is located in plenty of time to learn about special requirements.

Obtaining Licensure in More Than One State

When you graduate from pharmacy school, you can become licensed in the state where you attended school as well as in the state where you are completing a residency—giving you two original licenses. Otherwise, when you are licensed in one state and you move to another where you are not licensed, you must reciprocate your license to the new state from your original license—and you have to keep the original license paid and active throughout your career as a practicing pharmacist. If you reciprocate your license, you actually have two or more license payments annually.

For example, a student from Minnesota obtains a residency in Texas. She takes the NAPLEX and does a NAPLEX score transfer to Texas. She registers for and takes the MPJE exam in Texas and Minnesota. Now she has two original licensures and can use either of them later in her life to reciprocate if she decides to practice in a state other than Texas or Minnesota.

The only pharmacy residency programs that don't require licensure in a particular state are federal ones, such as the Indian Health Service and Veterans Administration. They stipulate only that you must be licensed in one state, no matter where you practice.

There are some benefits of obtaining licensure in two states when you are about to start a residency:

- Taking the MPJE in the state you graduated from may be easier because you've taken a law class and have been practicing in the state during your rotations.

- If you are considering returning to the state after completing your residency program, it's good to have an original license.

- If you obtain a job in the state where you complete your residency, you will have an original license there, too.

- This gives you flexibility if you practice in a third state later on and have to reciprocate your license; you can pay to keep the cheaper of the two licenses as your original license.

There are two downsides to the two-license approach:

- You incur an additional up-front cost.

- You have to take more than one MPJE exam.

Obtaining licensure in more than one state is fairly easy when you are first becoming licensed. You sign up for the NAPLEX and MPJE exams as you did for the first state you wanted to become licensed in. You then register for a NAPLEX score transfer and the additional MPJE. You only take the NAPLEX once, but you must take the additional MPJE for the second state and have your score transferred.

Downtime

After you've made it through graduation and taken your licensing exams, it's important to relax and have fun. After six or more challenging years of school, you've earned it. Soon you'll start an intense year in which you'll work more than eight hours a day and have little free time on weekends. You might be tempted to work long hours before your residency to earn extra spending money, but build in some rest time so you start your residency refreshed. Here's the typical timeline:

- Graduation – middle of May

- Licensing exams – end of May/beginning of June

- Moving – end of June

- Residency start date – July 1 or thereabouts

If you have to pack up and move to your new residency site, you'll only have a few weeks of downtime, so make the most of it. I know people who have used this time to take a cruise, road trip, or bicycle trip, backpack in the Appalachian mountains, get married, travel overseas, or kick back with family. What you do is your personal choice—but remember, it's really the last summer you'll have when you're not working.

Connecting with Your Residency

When the Match process is complete, you will receive a welcome email from your residency director. As soon as you have time, start reaching out to your co-residents, whether by Facebook, email, or phone. Try to set up a time to meet before the residency starts. It helps to get to know these people as soon as you can, because they will go through residency with you and will become your confidants, allies, and friends.

Send a brief email to your residency director asking how you can best prepare and what you are required to do before you begin your residency. Express how excited you are for the opportunity to work with this particular residency program. Even if it wasn't your top choice in the Match, be enthusiastic. You are going to have a great year! It can also be helpful to get in touch with the current residents and preceptors to ask about moving, the city, and other special recommendations they have from firsthand experience. See the list of suggestions and questions in the next section.

Moving

If you're moving to a new city or state for your residency, you face exciting changes—and you probably feel some anxiety, too. To make the transition easier, consider the following tips.

- Be organized in your packing, and label everything well so you can unpack quickly.

- Contact the current residents and preceptors at your new residency program and ask questions:

    ○ Which areas of town are good to live in?

    ○ Where do most residents live?

    ○ What is the typical rent that you pay?

    ○ What areas should be avoided?

    ○ What are the names of grocery chains for shopping? (This can be different across the country.)

    ○ Do you recommend any apartments/homes for rent?

- ○ Do you know of any good housing websites?

- ○ What fun activities are within/near the city?

- ○ Are there any bars/restaurants that you recommend trying?

- ○ Who are the Internet/cable providers in the area and which one is good?

- ○ What will I need to survive winter/summer (if moving to a new climate)?

- ○ What is the name of a good veterinarian (if you have a pet)?

- ○ Who is your dentist/optometrist?

- ○ How reliable is mass transit? Can I use mass transit to get to work?

- ○ What gym do you belong to or recommend?

- Start connecting with the other residents who will be in your residency class.

  - ○ Get to know each other a little.

  - ○ See if anyone wants or needs a roommate.

  - ○ Plan a fun activity or a time to hang out when you all arrive in town.

- Decide if you want a roommate.

- Transfer prescriptions and have at least one refill remaining.

- Research banks in the area (you may need to transfer banks; not all banks are national).

- Research fitness clubs in the area that will be close to you.

- Research special activities and attributes of the town you will be moving to, such as:

  - ○ Yearly festivals.

  - ○ Must-see attractions.

- ○ Local sports teams.

- ○ Restaurants.

- ○ School districts (if you have children).

- ○ Reliable mechanics/car dealerships.

It is smart to move to the city a week or so before you start your residency program, so that you have time to unpack and get familiar with the surroundings. If you are unable to pack all your belongings in your car or don't have family or friends who can help you move, consider using a moving company. These can be costly, but worth it if you have no other way of transporting your stuff. The best way to find a reliable mover is to ask for recommendations from people who have recently moved. Get estimates from more than one company and check the Better Business Bureau for any complaints or claims made against the company. Also, verify that the moving company is registered with the Federal Motor Carrier Safety Administration and has the proper licensing and insurance.

If you need to furnish a new apartment or house, many websites, such as www.craigslist.com, offer used items for sale or trade.

Finances

The end of pharmacy school can be costly if you are not prepared for it. You must pay to become licensed and may need to pay moving fees and other miscellaneous expenses before you get your first paycheck from the residency. Sidebar 10-3 lists items to budget for in your transition from student to resident.

Loan Payments

Once you graduate from pharmacy school, you will likely have some type of debt or loans. While taking part in your residency, you have options for dealing with your loan payments. Start by getting in touch with your lender. Ask about the following:

Sidebar 10-3. Items in Your Budget between Graduation and Start of Residency

- Licensing – $1200
  - NAPLEX – $485
  - MPJE – $200 (can be multiple if you are getting licensed in more than one state)
  - License application fee – varies by state ($0 to about $150)
  - Transcripts fee – varies by college ($0 to $25)
  - License cost – varies by state
- Moving expenses – from around $1000 to $3000
  - Gas – variable
  - Rental vehicle – variable
  - Movers – variable
  - Hotel stay (possibly) – variable
  - Food – variable
- Apartment down payment – $1000 or more
- Miscellaneous expenses for setting up an apartment or home – $500 to $700
- Meals
- New white coat – $30 to $45
- Scrubs (if your hospital allows you to wear them)
- New clothes (if so desired)
- Vacation (if so desired)
- New computer (if yours is old or failing)

- Can you consolidate your loans? If so, what is the interest rate? Sometimes you can shop around for a consolidating company. Look for the best interest rate and a program that doesn't penalize you if you want to pay off your loan early.

- When do your loan payments start? Some start immediately after graduation, while others start six months later.

- How does the lender calculate your loan payment? For example, is it based on your salary last year?

- What will your loan payment be? Is it affordable for you? If it isn't, is deferment/forbearance an option for you? Deferment means postponing your loan payment when interest is not accruing on subsidized loans. Forbearance means either postponing your loan payment, getting an agreement for a smaller payment, or extending your payment time—with interest accruing.

Deciding whether to start paying your loan amount or to go with deferment/forbearance is a personal choice based on your budget and the requirements of your lending institution. When I was in my residency, I was able to defer payments for some of my federal loans. I worked with the lender to get them all consolidated so that I had only one payment and the lowest interest rate possible. I couldn't defer payment on my private loans, however. The lender arranged for me to pay only the interest on the private loans, rather than making payments on the full principal plus interest. This allowed me to avoid paying interest on the interest I would have accumulated if I had deferred payment. When I had extra money, I put it toward the principal on my private loans.

Starting Your Residency

At the beginning of any residency program, it is common to feel overwhelmed. You'll sit through discussions about benefits, learn a new computer system, and meet many new people. And you'll face expectations the residency will have for you, even on the first day. Here are some simple "rules to live by" in those first days—and throughout your time as a resident.

- Hit the ground running.

- Have ideas about customizing your residency experience. What do you want to get out of it?

- Remember, you are in the program to learn, so that goal should be in your sights at all times.

- Be flexible.

- Become a master of time management.

- Learn to prioritize projects.

> Soon you'll start an intense year in which you'll work more than eight hours a day and have little free time on weekends.

- Do not be upset if you have to take work home and put in long hours; this is not a 9 to 5 job.

- Be open to new thoughts and ideas.

- Do not expect hand holding; become independent.

- Learn to set your own goals and deadlines.

- Improve your skills for communicating with a variety of audiences.

- Be open to constructive feedback; it helps you learn and grow.

- Find a healthy stress reliever that you can employ during residency, whether it's doing yoga, meditating for 10 minutes daily, or taking a walk each morning.

- Start using a budget, which reduces the stress of living with a modest salary.

- Create a timeline and to-do list to help you stay on track with both short-term and long-term projects. Continually review your to-do list and timeline.

- Do not procrastinate.

- Make friends with your co-residents.

- Don't lose sight of your final goal.

- Have FUN!

Conclusion

You are truly fortunate to be embarking on such a great learning experience. It will be one of the most memorable years of your life, filled with challenges, good times, new friends, and amazing professional growth. You can do it. Good luck!

Appendix

Helpful Checklists

The following checklists are supplied to help ensure that you don't overlook important tasks and that you're prepared for key events in the residency application process.

Midyear Clinical Meeting Residency Showcase Checklist

☐ Prepared list of questions

☐ My curriculum vitae (CV) is updated

☐ Copies of my CV to handout

☐ Business cards printed and packed

☐ Showcase map printed

☐ List of programs I must see

☐ Strategy planned for meeting with my programs of interest

☐ I know when all the programs I'm interested in are showing

☐ I know the names of residency directors at my programs of interest

☐ I have a sheet of notes on all of my top programs

☐ Comfortable walking shoes packed

☐ Lip balm packed

☐ Bottle of water

☐ Pens

- [ ] Paper or pad to take notes on
- [ ] Breath mints
- [ ] Kleenex
- [ ] Professional bag (not the free one handed out)

Residency Application Submission Checklist

- [ ] CV updated
    - ○ Ensure that all tracked changes are removed
    - ○ No spelling errors
    - ○ All names are correct
    - ○ PDF copy made
- [ ] Letter of intent written
    - ○ No spelling or grammar errors
    - ○ It tells your story
    - ○ It answers key questions about why you're interested in this program and the skills you will bring to it
    - ○ Sign your letter
- [ ] Letters of recommendations are being sent
- [ ] Transcript
- [ ] Supplemental materials are prepared (if any are required)

Interview Preparation Checklist

- [ ] Pen and paper
- [ ] Question list
- [ ] Notes about program and preceptors
- [ ] Notes about skills and experiences you want to highlight
- [ ] Water bottle
- [ ] Small snack
- [ ] Tide to Go stain stick (in case of mishaps)
- [ ] Program contact information
- [ ] Itinerary
- [ ] Driving directions (if required)
- [ ] Presentation slides (my copy)
- [ ] Presentation handout (for the audience)
- [ ] Flash drive with presentation
- [ ] Cellphone silenced (right before entering the building)
- [ ] CV reviewed before interview

Index

Note: Page numbers followed by *f* or *t* indicate figures or tables, respectively.

A

C

Index

G

H

I

J

K

Q

R